WHY WE GET SICK:
the Origins of Illness and Anxiety

Why We Get Sick: the Origins of Illness and Anxiety

A Practical Guide to Psychosomatic Medicine

J. A. Winter, M.D.

FOREWORD BY WILLIAM S. KROGER, M.D.

Weathervane Books
New York

FOREWORD

In the last fifty years, tremendous strides have been made in the practice of medicine. For instance, until recently, the idea that a physical disease such as an ulcer of the stomach could be due partially to upset emotions was considered utterly fantastic. Today, emotional instability as one of the factors for causation of disease has proved a useful concept for the preponderance of human ailments. Fortunately, this idea—the psychosomatic approach—has gained almost full acceptance from even skeptical physicians as well as a dubious laity.

It is surprising how many sophisticated persons consider that the term psychosomatic means psychologic or psychogenic. Actually, it refers to the interaction and interdependence of emotional and physical factors in the production of symptoms. Thus, it is no wonder that the modern physician no longer resorts to an "either/or" but, rather, a "both/and" approach.

No longer can it be disputed that thoughts based on harmful and buried memories can upset the delicate adjustments which help maintain the equilibrium of the bodily processes. Nor is there any doubt that many patients present themselves to their physicians with symptoms which tend to express their deep-seated emotional conflicts. Since many believe that their symptoms have a physical basis for their existence, neurotic conflicts are perpetuated. This frequently is what the sufferer desires, as it obviates facing an unpleasant life situation.

Dr. Winters lucidly explains how numerous symptomatic manifestations are the result of the organs "voicing" their protest in a manner which becomes intelligible only if one listens, understands and heeds their "language." Inasmuch as the healing arts have become more constricted and divided into various disciplines, even the well-trained specialist has not been able to practice psychosomatic or comprehensive medicine. This is not to imply that such a dual approach will solve all illnesses of mankind—it will not. However, as Dr. Winters so admirably points out, neglecting the both-sides-of-the-street approach to the understanding and treatment of disease processes can seriously impair recovery.

The author of this volume is well aware that the recuperative powers reside, in part, in the patient. He describes what the latter can do about tapping these "forgotten assets." Dr. Winters stresses that the patient gets himself sick by continually bombarding his psyche by negative, destructive thoughts to produce a bewildering array of anxieties and tensions which lead to psychosomatic disorders. Thus, it is obvious that reversal of these unhealthy processes by a sort of "scientific power of positive thinking" should prove most effective in alleviating the preponderance of illnesses falling into the classification of "psychosomatic."

Dr. Winters not only gives the why, when and how we develop symptoms, but also tells us what to do about them. On the basis of his vast clinical experience, he describes how we can recognize whether or not our symptoms are psychosomatic. His thesis is that increased susceptibility to positive therapeutic suggestions can be attained by relaxation and concentration which produce greater receptivity, self-objectivity and richer understanding of the need for one's symptoms.

Dr. Winters also explains how the organism is continually interacting in a field of forces produced by environmental factors. As a result, he places particular emphasis on verbal communication processes and their relevance for producing and relieving anxiety-provoking tensions. He also is well aware that even though mind and body cannot be separated, the former can be influenced by communications from within and without the organism to nullify those noxious stimuli which lead to psychosomatic disorders.

To one who has practiced psychosomatic medicine for over 30 years, it is not surprising that sexual problems such as frigidity and impotence are commonly the *raison d'etre* for a wide variety of psychosomatic disorders. The skillful handling of these problems by Dr. Winters is in line with modern dynamic psychiatric principles. He is to be complimented on making what ordinarily are complicated explanations extraordinarily simple to understand.

The author and publisher are to be congratulated for bringing out another edition of this fascinating and timely book destined to become the "bible" of those interested in psychosomatic medicine. I consider it a distinct honor to have the privilege of writing the foreword to this epochal book.

WILLIAM S. KROGER, M.D.*

Beverly Hills, California

* Past-President, Academy of Psychosomatic Medicine; Consulting Editor in Psychosomatics, Western Journal Surgery, Obstetrics & Gynecology.

CONTENTS

CONTENTS

It has often been said that there is nothing new under the sun. Certainly, human beings aren't new, and there is nothing particularly startling or original about "troubles." "Psychomatic," however, is a word that is so new that it is in only the most recent dictionaries, and it means, of course, "pertaining to both the mind and the body."

Treating illness from this point of view seems to have considerable advantages over some of the older methods. A human being is a person first of all; sometimes he becomes a sick person. Too often we, as medical men, rush in to treat the ailment or the disease by itself, losing sight of the fact that the patient is a person, and that being sick is only one part of his living. True, it often seems to threaten his whole living, but our profession would dwindle rapidly if he did not also have at his disposal the means of being well.

Out of this there comes a sort of paradox, which is what this book concerns itself with—the paradox that people mistakenly seek to solve the problems of existence and survival by becoming ill.

As developed in this book, it turns out not to be such a paradox after all. Some explanations are suggested, but, more important, practical means are offered for an understanding of illness and some ways of overcoming it.

We are going to discuss things in this book that you might never have heard before; you will also read statements that are so obvious that it may seem that we are insulting your intelligence. There will be discussions of the results of laborious scientific experiments; there will also be discussions of old wives' tales, of superstition and of folk-lore.

It would be easier, therefore, to say what this book isn't, rather than what it is going to be. In the first place this book will *not* be a substitute for the attentions of your family physician. On the contrary, many of the concepts and techniques which will be discussed can be used only by one who has had considerable training in the healing arts. Yet we feel that you should know about them, for with this knowledge you will be better able to work with your doctor when or if the necessity should arise.

Nor is it intended that this book will enable you to become a practitioner of psychosomatic medicine. After all, you don't become an automobile mechanic simply because you know how an internal combustion engine works. It's a good idea to know something about your car, however, because you are better able to detect changes in function and to determine whether or not they demand immediate attention. So it will be with this book. We propose to give you an idea of psychosomatic disease in order that you will be able to suspect it—and then to consult one who is trained to recognize it and to treat it in the most effectual way. We hope, however, that there will be much which you can learn to use for yourself.

WHY WE GET SICK:
the Origins of Illness and Anxiety

CHAPTER I

WHAT IS "PSYCHOSOMATIC"?

In all the writings which have appeared since the dawn of history the idea has prevailed that there is a body and there is a mind, and that they are two separate things. The concept is such an old one that no one knows how it developed.

It has been suggested that the idea of a "soul" or "spirit" or "psyche," as the Greeks called it, or "ka," as the Egyptians called it, may have originated even as early as prehistoric man. Someone has suggested that a cave man lay down to sleep in his cave and dreamed, and that during this dream he hunted the sabre-tooth tiger, killing it and dragging it home to his cave. In the morning when he awoke he asked his wife (or perhaps one of his wives) what happened to the tiger he had killed.

"What tiger?" she asked.

"The one I killed last night."

"You weren't hunting last night. I got up before dawn to fix the fire and you were snoring like a cave bear. If you'd do more hunting and less sleeping, your family would be better off. Why, I'm still wearing last year's wolfskins."

At this point the cave man, like his more modern descendants, probably closed his ears to his wife's tirade and thought about more important things. How could he explain this? He felt as if he had been hunting; he could remember everything that happened; yet the evidence of his senses and of the senses of others now told him that he hadn't left the cave all night.

It's possible for us to understand how a primitive mind might try to explain this. There must be a part of the person which is free to separate itself from the tangible flesh of the body, and to go wandering off. Of course, the savage couldn't see this thing—it was invisible, not material.

But wait—how about the breath? He couldn't see the stuff he breathed, and yet breathing was associated with living. If you didn't breathe, you didn't live. Maybe this "spirit" thing was something like the breath.

We moderns know that there was an identification in the primitive mind between "breath" and "soul"—the Greek word "psyche" once meant breath; the Latin word "spiritus" appears in such words as "expiration" and "inspiration," both of which apply to the act of breathing.

This concept of "spirit," as you can see, is a rather simple one, easily grasped by a primitive mind. Of course, it isn't completely explanatory, and there are many mysterious aspects—but the whole physical universe presents so many mysterious and inexplicable facets to the primitive mentality that one mystery more or less isn't important.

You can also see how a slightly more agile mind can broaden this concept of the "spirit." A person can dream of dying, and awake to find that he is still alive, or he can dream of the dead, and they appear as they did when they were living. It would follow, therefore, that the spirit is immortal, that it is only the body which dies, leaving the spirit to persist in its intangible, out-of-this-world existence.

It is on this concept of "spirit" as differentiated from body that most of our religions are based. Some religions aver that a "spirit," when it is separated by death from its fleshy envelope, can move on to another body, to be reincarnated as another human or as an animal. Other religions suggest that the "spirit" moves on to another plane of existence, there to receive the rewards or punishments which were not forthcoming during its earthly existence.

There is no quarrel with this idea. It is one which is almost universally accepted, so much so, in fact, that it is only with the greatest intellectual effort that one can think in any other way. The concept of spirit or soul or psyche is a basic idea in our thinking about ourselves—it is so basic, so firmly fixed a part of knowledge, that we often forget that its existence can neither be proved or disproved.

Our living includes the process of constantly testing (or "proving") our knowledge, and we make these tests by comparing our intellectual ideas with our sensation facts.

There are some things which we can test, some which can't be tested.

It is difficult to see how we could prove, by a sensory experience, the existence of a "mind." We can't prove the existence of atoms, either—but what happened at Hiroshima and Nagasaki shows that, if there aren't atoms, there are things which act mightily like atoms are supposed to act.

In this book, then, we shall regard the idea of a separate entity of "soul" or "spirit" as an unproved assumption. It may be correct, it may not.

Let's see if there isn't some other way in which we can speak about the body and the mind, a way which may also be correct or incorrect, but which seems to have a practical application to the well-being of mankind. Let's try to find out if there isn't a way of viewing the body/mind concept which can be tested by our own sensory experiences. If we can do so, we might find a better means of explaining human behavior.

To discuss this new concept we might start out by making an analogy. Suppose that you went into a room where there was a steel shaft protruding from one wall and that the shaft was rotating steadily. You could study this rotation; you could count the number of revolutions per minute which the shaft made; you could attach weights to it and see if the r.p.m.'s increased or decreased; you could try to stop it and see if it would start again. You could do all these things and many more without having the least idea of what was causing the rotation, whether the

4

shaft were turned by an electric motor, a steam engine, a squirrel in a cage or by the same agency which turned Joshua's wheel.

We could, in other words, study the *function* of rotation, without knowing anything about the *structure* which is rotating. We also note that we cannot have one without the other; there cannot be the function of rotation without a structure to rotate, and a structure that does not function is, in a sense, dead.

We apply these words of "function" and "structure" to our view of the human body and the human mind. We shall use the word "body" to apply to the *structure* of a person—to the muscles, bones, organs, nerve cells, to all of the little structures which make up the human being. When we use the word "mind," we shall refer to the *function* of this structure or any part of it. "Mental" will, therefore, pertain to function, also; in the sense in which this word will be used in this book, the act of emptying the bladder is a mental function, as are seeing, hearing, feeling, imagining and every other act of which the human is capable.

You might ask what is to be gained by twisting the word "mind" out of its common usage in this fashion. Why not use another word entirely? The reason for so doing is to establish a bridge, as it were, between the old usage and the new. The word "mind" is a good word, and it is used quite accurately. For example, a doctor will occasionally examine a patient and be unable to discover any definite structural changes in any of the organs; there is the ten-

5

dency then to tell the patient that his illness is all in his mind. Most people resent that statement, as they interpret it to mean that their troubles are imaginary, hence unreal, and that the doctor thinks that they are deliberately malingering.

In the sense in which we shall use the word "mind" in this book, however, the diagnosis that "it's *all* in your mind" is not quite an accurate one since the doctor means, "Your troubles are due to a disorder of function, and there don't seem to be any structural changes to account for them."

There are other uses of the word "mind" which tie in the old with the new, giving a new significance to the old usage: take the expression "it slipped my mind," used as a phrase to mean, "I forgot." In our use of the word, we would say that the forgotten experience has slipped out of the mind—it has temporarily ceased to be a usable function. We might also point out that forgetting is a "mental" function, too, one which is often deliberate.

With the understanding that, in this book, the word "mind" equals function, we are ready to take the first step in defining the word "psychosomatic." We can say that a psychosomatic illness is one in which changes in function predominate over changes in structure. This is not to say that there can't be any changes of structure in a psychosomatic illness; we consider an ulcer of the stomach to be a typical example of a psychosomatic illness, and there certainly are structural changes with this condition—changes which are observable by means of the X-ray, the gastro-

6

scope (which is an instrument with which the interior of the stomach can be visualized) or at the time of surgery. The structural changes seem to follow the functional changes, however; the change in function seems to occur first, and this, in turn, seems to give rise to the alteration of structure.

There are some other aspects of psychosomatic disease which should be discussed before we can reach a thorough understanding. In order to discuss them we must first clarify the concept of the adequate stimulus and the appropriate response.

Supposing that someone were to hit you on the head with a baseball bat; the chances are excellent that you would develop a headache shortly thereafter. This would be an example of an adequate stimulus followed by an appropriate response. The blow on the head would be a sufficiently injurious stimulus to produce the response of headache, and the headache would be a common enough response to the injury to make it probable, or appropriate.

But suppose that someone said to you, "You're stupid!" and that you thereupon developed a headache. In this case the stimulus is inadequate, because the pattern of sound waves which we interpret as the message "you're stupid" do not in themselves constitute an injury. And yet you are responding to this stimulus as if it were adequate, and are hence making an inappropriate response; you would be making the same response to a pattern of the sound waves of "you're stupid" as you would to a definite injury, and it is obvious that they are not the same.

It is our contention that at some time in your life the two *were* the same, in that they occurred at the same time. In other words, we suggest that at some one or more times in your life the words "you're stupid" and the sensation which we call headache *did* occur simultaneously and thereby became equivalent.

This reaction can also be explained in another way. This second explanation is probably more important than the first, in that it seems to be the mechanism which is operating in the majority of cases. It has to do with the emotional response to stimuli, and with the reactions which follow emotional changes. We suggest that there was a time when you were angry and had a headache—that you have learned, as it were, that headache and anger go together. The phrase "you're stupid" can provike the reaction of anger; but anger is equivalent to headache, so you can either get angry or have a headache. In our society the demonstration of anger is not encouraged but is frowned upon; it is, in a sense, easier or safer to get a headache than it is to become angry—and so the headache develops.

This discussion of the role of emotion in psychosomatic illnesses is only to introduce the concept. There will be a more thorough discussion of it later in the book.

To return to the discussion of the inappropriate response to the inadequate stimulus: we note that the response is inappropriate in the framework of the Here and the Now, that the stimulus does not seem to be adequate Here and Now—but that there is a strong possibility that there *was* a time when the stimulus and the response were coexistent.

For example, a child may have pulled the cat's tail and the cat scratched him. The object called "cat" would be associated with the pain of a scratch—and dislike of the cat, which in this experience is equivalent to pain, is appropriate. It is not appropriate for an adult to dislike a cat simply because he was scratched by another cat twenty years ago; it indicates a confusion between cats and a confusion between times—and confusion is the essence of psychosomatic or psychic illness.

The fact that there is a confusion, however, is what enables us to treat the patient. It is obviously true that a person learns by experience and only by experience. If he confuses the cat of today, which does not cause pain, with the cat of twenty years ago, which did cause pain, we can help him as a patient to a re-evaluation of cats. We do this by assisting him to recall and re-experience the sensations of the event in which cat and pain were made equivalent—and by so doing this fixed relationship is dissolved. This point also will be discussed at greater length elsewhere.

At this point it becomes possible to say what constitutes a psychosomatic illness. We define a psychosomatic disease as an illness with the following characteristics:

1. The disorder is one of function, rather than of structure, although structural changes may occur later.
2. It is precipitated by an inadequate stimulus.
3. The response is not appropriate to the stimulus.
4. It is based on some past experience, usually painful.
5. It is based on fixed associations—a certain stimulus will almost always elicit an unvarying response.

6. There seems to be a lack of awareness of Here and Now; the patient's reactions seem to overlook or ignore the present-time situation in favor of some previously-experienced one.

Now let's see if we can't say the same thing in more simple words, eliminating the scientific terminology. We can say that, in a psychosomatic disease, a person may look healthy at first glance; he *acts* sick, however—and we can't see any good reason for such actions. Later on, after he has been ill for some time, there might be changes which can be observed medically. There illnesses seem to arise from problem-situations and from words, rather than from actual injuries, or infection. The ill person often doesn't act as we might expect him to act—he's more apt to behave as a child would. We can usually find that he had a similar illness in the past, and that he acted during that illness in the way he is acting now. We also notice that the ill person's actions are fixed and unchanging—when he gets angry, he always has a headache; when he is unhappy, he always over-eats; when he doesn't eat, he always gets a pain in his stomach. Finally, the sick person acts as if he didn't care about what was going on outside of him; he's much more concerned with his ideas and thoughts then he is with the sensations of Here and Now.

It should be clearly understood that this list is incomplete, in that we can speak of psychosomatic illnesses in many, many other ways besides those mentioned here. These are not the *only* distinguishing points, nor is our viewpoint the *only* way of looking at the problem; there are other ways, equally valid. This is only *one* way of speaking about the subject, a way which has been chosen because it has led to increased understanding of illness and increased ability to alleviate illness.

And what are considered to be psychosomatic illnesses? First, let us consider the various conditions which are classified as psychosomatic by other workers in the field. There are, of course, a good many books on the subject, of which we mention only a few.

Dr. H. Flanders Dunbar, in her book, *Mind and Body*, mentions such diseases as the allergies, the common cold, tuberculosis, hysterical blindness, arthritis, coronary heart disease, rheumatic heart disease, high blood pressure, obesity, peptic ulcer, migraine, diabetes, colitis, asthma, hay fever—all of which, she feels, are either of psychosomatic origin or are associated with "mental" and emotional disturbances.

To this list Dr. Franz Alexander adds constipation, painful menstruation, epilepsy, goiter, frigidity, impotence, false pregnancy, paroxysmal tachycardia (which is the medical term for the condition wherein the heart suddenly begins to beat extremely rapidly) and hives.

With these lists we are in complete agreement. We might even go so far as to add a few more diseases, including Parkinson's disease (paralysis agitans), multiple sclerosis and cancer. We don't *know* with any great degree of certainty that these are of psychosomatic origin, nor do we know the degree of emotional involvement—there has not yet been the time or opportunity for making an exhaustive investigation. We suspect, however, that using the approach of psychotherapy might be helpful in these conditions. Certainly the conventional medical and surgical forms of treatment leave much to be desired, as any doctor will admit.

To sum up, then, we can say that *any* disease is, to some extent, psychosomatic in origin, that in any disease, no matter what the obvious cause, there are psychosomatic aspects.

CHAPTER II

THE IMPORTANCE OF BEING ILL

WHY WE GET SICK

EVERY illness has a cause. Every illness is a result of some sort of contact with something in the world which is outside of the body. The contact may be with bacteria in contaminated water, with an object which is extremely hot or extremely cold, or with a switch wielded by an angry parent or with the voice of an angry parent—but there must be contact.

But—and here is one of the observations on which psychosomatic medicine is based—*the contact doesn't have to be now.* You can get a stomach-ache today because you ate some spoiled food today; you are also able to get a stomach-ache today because you ate some spoiled food ten years ago.

We don't expect you to accept these statements just because they're made here. But there is a reason for making the statements. Let's leave them for a while and show later why we make them.

The process of living is the process of coming in contact with our environment. We interact with the environment; there is no other way to live except to interact.

As an example, we have to breathe in air in order to live. The air is part of our environment; so is our food. We move through our environment. We live in our environment; there is no escaping this fact.

Usually this contact with our environment is easy and painless; if so, we call it health. We can also call it growth.

What, then, is illness? Where does illness fit into the picture?

We suggest that illness, also, is an interaction between us and our environment. It is a natural process, a part of growth and change. True, it is a "mistake"—but only in the sense that it is not the *only* process. We might even say that it is a way of becoming healthy.

It may sound absurd at first to say that health and illness are similar. We know that they are different—but what makes the difference?

Consider this: we know that it's necessary to have food in order to grow and be healthy, but that if we overeat we get sick. We need sunshine—but too much sun makes us sick.

In other words, we need to interact with our environment—but the rate and type of reaction make the difference between being healthy and being ill.

We all try to control the rate of our reactions with the world outside us. We call this control adaptation, and the more successfully we adapt, the healthier we are.

This seems to be a part of the natural order of things. As we come in contact with our environment we adapt to it. There are various ways in which we can adapt, some of which seem to be more successful, some apparently less successful. Sometimes we make changes in the environment, sometimes we ourselves have to change.

As an illustration of this, take our adaptation to the disease called malaria. Malaria results when a certain micro organism is planted in our bodies by the bite of a mosquito. We don't seem to be able to live comfortably with the malaria parasite, so we make our adaptation by eliminating the parasite with quinine and atabrine, and by eliminating the breeding places of the mosquito.

We adapt to the disease called small-pox in a different way. We have found that by deliberately inoculating ourselves with another disease called cow-pox or vaccinia and becoming ill with it, we can adapt ourselves to small-pox without any sign of illness.

Illness, therefore, is a method of adapting oneself to one's environment.

Let's see how this applies to the newborn baby. For the previous nine months he has been getting his oxygen supply through the umbilical cord. Suddenly he is thrust into the world, his cord is severed and he is now responsible for his own breathing. He appears distressed by this—he often turns a livid blue, chokes and wails a protest. We could say that he is sick. We could also say that he is in the process of adapting himself to a change in his environment.

Again, let us watch a young baby when he is learning to eat solid food. All his previous experience had been that food was a liquid, given by means of a nipple. Now he has something solid in his mouth—and he spits it out. The mother is worried; the baby is sick—he won't eat.

Of course, there's another complication here: by this time he is able to detect emotional changes in his mother, and this spitting out of food is thereby given an additional value. But more of this later.

Yes, we can say that the baby is sick; but we can also say that he is in the process of learning how to cope with something new in his environment—solid food. He is learning how to deal with this new form of nutriment in terms of chewing, swallowing and digesting. This sort of learning is growth, too.

Take another example—suppose a man breaks his leg. He is sick—but he is also dealing with a new situation, a real situation to which he is adapting. On this level of activity the cause of his fracture is relatively unimportant. No matter what the cause, the cells which have to do with bone repair are busily at work, restoring his leg bone to its previous ability to function. He is, in short, going through a natural process of adaptation—at least natural to the circumstances.

16

Still another example: suppose that you get a splinter in your hand. After a few days of slight soreness you will see the formation of pus; an abscess will form, which will rupture and discharge both the pus and the splinter. In this case you are adapting to the splinter by isolating it. The pus contains thousands of white blood cells, which devour the bacteria which entered with the splinter; these white cells also eat their way toward the skin surface, making an opening through which the splinter can be expelled. The abscess isn't too comfortable—but it's one means—a natural means—of dealing with a foreign body.

We could give many more examples of illness and show how disease can be looked upon as a process of adaptation. We might mention some of the "popular" illnesses, where people seem to get sick just because others are getting sick, because it is "the thing to do." But this, too, is a process of adaptation, this time to the people of our environment, rather than to bacteria or viruses.

To sum up, in this section we are trying to point out that illness is a natural process. It must be kept firmly in mind, however, that health is an equally natural process. Instead of setting up a rigid contrast between sickness and health, let us consider that these are but two faces of the same coin.

We present this point of view because we find that getting a clearer picture of our problem puts us in a better position to handle it. We therefore ask that you think this over: you may discover that this attitude towards illness can be helpful in developing a more reasonable outlook on health.

Let us go back to our example of the man who had the broken leg. Picture him in the hospital; his leg is in a plaster cast, perhaps with a weight or two attached to it by means of an ingenious system of pulleys. He gets attention from the attending physician, from the intern, from the nurse, from the orderly. His wife comes in to see him as often as she can, and is careful not to do anything or say anything which might disturb him. His slightest whims are met. To use the army expression, "He never had it so good."

Contrast this with his usual life, when his day starts with a hasty breakfast and a dash to the office, where he is often in conflict with the boss, the customers or his fellow-workers.

How much incentive does he have for getting well?

Or consider the child who has a cold. When such an illness occurs, he is freed from the responsibility of going to school; he lies in bed while his mother waits on him. Of course, he is not too comfortable—but he is also given pleasures which he doesn't ordinarily get. Why should he get better fast?

He does recover, of course; the human organism will accept just so much of these specious pleasures of illness— but the temptation to use illness as an acceptable means of avoiding duties also develops from just such experiences.

This is the pleasure side of illness. This is the sort of experience which attracts one towards illness. There are other types of situations which keep us in illness because we are not permitted to be anything else but ill.

The example of this is the patient who had had asthma for forty years. He consulted a doctor who used the psychosomatic approach, and at one point the doctor told him that he didn't have to have asthma.

Said the patient, "You know, doctor, I've had hundreds of doctors tell me I *had* asthma, but you're the first who told me that I didn't have to have it."

In other words, there seems to be a lot of illness which persists because the possibility of recovery is not mentioned. The patient is told he is sick, that he has a disease, that he has all kinds of symptoms—but where is the statement that he can recover, that he will recover?

When you stop to think about it, you can easily see that all of us have had a lot of training in obedience. We do as we are told—a lesson frequently administered, often reinforced with the pain of punishment or the pleasure of approval. So when the doctor says you have asthma, and if you're a good, obedient boy or girl, you have asthma. And if the doctor neglects to suggest that you can recover from asthma, it is entirely possible that you may continue to have it.

There is another aspect of this. Supposing that you have learned to fear a certain disease, such as cancer; supposing also that you observe in yourself one of the signs of cancer. This sign may also be related to numerous other diseases— but in your mental patterns of response it means cancer. If you are completely convinced you have this disease, then you will act as if you have the disease—and you may die of fear ever though you don't die of cancer.

This ability of the human being to convince himself of the reality of his fears has been known for a long time. There is the classic case of the unpopular teacher whose students decided to play a prank on him. They dragged him out of bed in the middle of the night, took him to where they had set up a guillotine. They blindfolded his eyes, made him kneel with his head in the place where the axe would fall. Then one of these playful students drew a piece of ice across the back of the teacher's neck, quickly following it with warm water. The teacher promptly died— convinced that he had been beheaded.

If this is possible, can't it be equally possible to be convinced of the presence of a disease? Could it not be that one was so well-convinced through fear that he continued to act as if he had the disease, thereby repressing the natural healing process?

There's another reason for staying sick: the fear of recovery. It may be the sort of emotion expressed as, "I'm afraid I'll have to go back to work tomorrow." It may be even more subtle than that, as in the case of the man who had had a heart attack. He had seen several cases of this before in his family and friends, and in each case the person seemed to become markedly better just before he died. With this sort of information, why should the man get better? In his experience, getting better is a fore-runner of death; it's just too risky to try to recover.

And let's look at this reason for persistent illness: sickness as a means of revenge. There was the case of the little boy who had been continually thwarted by his parents. His life was a constant bombardment of "Jimmy, don't do that!" "Be quiet!" "Go away—don't bother me." The child had no means of "getting even" in this situation; his parents were so much bigger and more powerful than he that he was helpless. He found out, however, that by coughing he could produce a very dramatic effect in his parents—and so he developed a chronic cough. It became especially worse whenever he was told to do something that he didn't want to do, such as going to bed or going to sleep.

Of course, we could say that this cough was a means of getting attention; that's one aspect of it. We can also say that by coughing he was able to get rid of some of the excess energy which had not found free expression because of his parents' restrictions.

It should be emphasized here that no one of these "reasons" for remaining ill is sufficient all by itself to keep a person in a state of ill-health. It requires numerous experiences, this one dragging you in one direction, that one pushing you in another direction, to produce the resultant which is chronic sickness. One obviously irrational reason for staying sick is seldom enough; when there are numerous reasons, they are effective by sheer weight of numbers. The "reasons" could be rejected one at a time, but when they are present in a huge mass—well, it's harder to fight.

Why are we telling you all this? We do so to show how using illness as a means of escape from responsibility, as a type of obedience, as a means of revenge, because of a fear of recovery—in short, when a person uses illness as a successful pattern of adaptation, he is distorting a natural function. This pseudo-successful distortion, in turn, leads to a behavior pattern which often becomes the *only* way of adapting.

In most cases of chronic illness we see that rigidly-patterned behavior is repeated over and over. It looks as if the patient had the habit of staying sick—but he doesn't have to keep the habit.

It speaks well for our innate drive toward health that we recover as rapidly as we do. There is such a high value placed on illness that, for most people, it would seem to be a far wiser thing to be constantly ill. But yet we seem to know instinctively that we want to be well—the drive toward health and life, toward a truly satisfying interaction with our environment, can always be stronger than the mistaken adaptation called illness.

WHY WE REPEAT OUR ILLNESSES

It doesn't take much observation to notice that most people have a definite pattern of illness, one which they play over and over. There's the woman who says, "I just know that I'm going to get one of my headaches again." There's the man who announces (and somewhat proudly, too), "I just can't stand to look at a bright light—it always gives me a headache." And every mother will notice that her child will have a specific reaction of illness to some severe emotional stress.

We said that these people "play" their illnesses. We used that word to emphasize that the behavior-patterns of illness remind us of a phonograph record, which always and inevitably plays the same tune. And why shouldn't it? That's the way it was recorded in the first place.

We suspect that recurrent, habitual illnesses are a result of a sort of recording process. This recording process has many forms, one of which we call "memory."

Ordinarily when we speak of things remembered, we usually refer to events which we can recall. But there are other "memories," ones which are not easily recallable. Such "memories" make up the content of what various writers have called the unconscious, the subconscious, the reactive portion of the mind, and so on. They are recollection-recordings of what occurred during moments of stress, when the person was sick or in pain or in the grip of some violent emotion. These recordings seem to carry all sorts of information—the sensations, the actions, the words, the feelings.

You most likely have noticed something like this taking place at some time or other: a person suddenly becomes angry for some apparently trivial reason. During his anger you might notice that he uses words which have nothing to do with the situation, that he takes actions which are entirely unnecessary and non-helpful to the problem at hand. If you're a careful observer, and have the chance to see this person in several spells of anger, you will hear the same words and see the same actions with each spell.

We think that this can best be explained by comparing

this with a recording—a recording labelled "This is what to do when you get angry." And every person has his own rack full of recordings which he plays again and again. And note, please, that he doesn't have to play these again—he just acts as if he had to.

You will also recall, when we remind you of it, that some people will say, "I feel as though I'm coming down with a cold," or "I just know that I'm going to be sick," or "I got my feet wet; now I'm going to have cramps," or "I'm going to that dance next week and, as usual, I'm starting to get pimples."

How do you suppose these people "know" that they're going to get a cold, or cramps, or pimples? Doesn't this sound like a record being played—an old familiar record which you can recognize after just the first few bars? And don't you also think that we could do without the re-playing of these records?

Of course, these illness-recordings which we have mentioned are trivial; but the major illnesses seem to follow the same sort of pattern.

In spite of this, no two illnesses are ever identical, either in the same person or in different persons. Every doctor learns that while he is still in medical school. When he studies a certain disease, such as appendicitis, he learns about the typical case: when he gets into the clinic, he soon finds out that there is no such thing as a typical case. The discovery of a case of appendicitis which is "just like the book" is a rare and exciting event.

This "record" theory is offered as a possible explanation

for the repetition of illness patterns. There are probably numerous other explanations, equally valid. This is, nonetheless, a useful explanation. Perhaps, if you consider it a little more, you will see how a person goes about creating a disease. And if *you* create the disease, when you become aware of it, you can also create health.

HOW TO OVERCOME PATTERNS OF ILLNESS

Several years ago a type of "mental" treatment enjoyed considerable popularity. It was originated by a French doctor named Coué, and consisted mainly in having the patients repeat such phrases as, "Every day in every way I'm getting better and better," and, "It's going, it's going" —referring to the unwanted symptom.

There were numerous "cures" reported, some of them quite dramatic. The medical profession in general tended to scoff at this method, calling it "faith healing," "pure hypnosis," "mass hysteria" and the like.

We are not going to defend Couéism, nor are we going to recommend it. We merely use this as an example of the fact that "cures" have been obtained when the person *says* he is getting better.

We mentioned before that we are all pretty well trained to obedience. We are so well-trained, in fact, that we even obey ourselves. When a person says, "I'm going to get sick," the chances of his getting sick are much greater than if he said, "I'm going to remain healthy."

But obedience implies much more than the mere repetition of words. Suppose you asked one of your children to take his hat off and he said, "Yes"—but still left his hat on his head? That would be only verbal obedience—which is meaningless.

You've seen that sort of thing lots of times. It's the sort of conduct seen in the alcoholic who "swears off" every morning and gets drunk again every night.

No, obedience requires more than verbal agreement; it requires *action*. And so we say that it isn't such a bad idea to say, "I'm not going to be sick any longer," but that you will reach your goal of health only if you take some sort of action. If you talk well and act sick, you will only magnify the confusion. If you act as if you are well, there's much less tendency to talk sick.

A variation of this idea has been used by the medical profession for a long time, although they wouldn't speak of it as psychotherapy. When a patient comes in with a sprained ankle, the doctor will inject the region of the sprain with procaine, which is a local anesthetic. Then he puts on some light supportive dressing of adhesive tape and tells the patient to go out and walk as if there were nothing wrong with him; the anesthetic, of course, permits this. Patients who do so find that the sprain heals up in just a few days; if they "baby" the sprain, lie in bed, hobble around on crutches, walk as if the foot were in danger of falling off at any minute, it takes weeks and weeks for the sprain to heal.

Undoubtedly the medication has some effect—but the acting as if not sick is important, too.

We discussed before the idea that a recurrent illness

acted like a record being played over. You might like to know how to keep the record from starting. It's not too difficult: by refraining from associating one sensation with an entire disease pattern you can prevent the activation of the disease.

To give an example, suppose that you suddenly feel chilly. You might say, "I feel cold," which is simply a report of the sensation. You might also say, "I feel as if I am getting a cold," in which case you are telling of your expectations of getting a disease. By reporting the sensation, there seems to be a tendency for it to remain a sensation, nothing more. By expecting a disease, it seems that you make the association between "cold" and "a cold"—and that starts the record labelled "How to get a cold."

You might even try to extend this process. If you feel chilly, just consider *why* you feel that way. Are you insufficiently clothed? Have you been exposed to a sudden drop in temperature? Is there something that you can do to overcome the feeling of chilliness, such as taking a hot drink, or putting on more bed-clothes or setting the thermostat higher? If so, you can do it.

The next step would be to think about the reasons for getting "a cold." Would there be any advantages to getting a respiratory illness at this time? What would happen if you got a cold? What would happen if you didn't get a cold? Such thinking often brings to light the possibility of a sort of deliberateness about becoming ill—and, of course, if you think that the best thing for you to do at this time is to get a cold, you can have one.

In doing this type of thinking one frequently runs into the phrase, "I wish." Those words have many meanings, one of which is, "I think I want this but I'm not going to take any action." You have a choice, then, of wishing to be healthy or being healthy.

In this discussion of the attitudes which might affect health, please note that we are *not* saying, "You must think this way," or, "Don't think that way." These are ways in which *you can think if you so desire.* They may be helpful to you, or they may not; that can be determined by trial.

There are a good many "self-help" books on the market in which the reader is given a list of "musts" and "don'ts." Perhaps his health will improve by these methods—but it seems more as if he were trying to be compulsively healthy. He is urged to force himself into a state of health. We do not believe that force is necessary, nor is it effective except to start another compulsion.

We have tried to show you ways in which you can think, with the understanding that by "thinking" we include the complete process of feeling, deciding and acting. Thinking, to be complete, requires action; if it doesn't include action, it's not thinking.

CHAPTER III

THE IMPORTANCE OF MAKING MISTAKES

THE MISTAKE AS A BASIC LEARNING PATTERN · THE MISTAKE
AS THE FOUNDATION OF THE INFERIORITY COMPLEX · THE
MISTAKE AS A BASIS OF THE "GUILT COMPLEX" · HOW TO
MAKE THE MOST OF OUR MISTAKES

THE MISTAKE AS A BASIC LEARNING PATTERN

Did you ever watch a baby learning how to play with a
string of beads? It's an experience you shouldn't miss, for
in his tiny, simple efforts to learn we can see, in miniature,
the learning process of the whole human race. We can see
how the baby learns to play with beads—and we can also
see how this learning process is repeated in the austere
laboratories of science.

29

Let's watch the baby and see what he does as he is learning. What steps can we see him take as he tries to learn more about beads? Well, the first step seems to be observation. For a long time the beads are merely a part of the background, one of the elements in a confused hodge-podge of colors and shapes. We might say that he is looking at the beads, but doesn't see them. Then suddenly he becomes aware of an object which has a certain regularity of pattern, a difference of color from the rest of the objects within his field of vision—he sees the beads.

Now he doesn't know that these are beads; he certainly doesn't know that this thing he is looking at is called "a string of beads." He just acts as if he wanted to do something with this new thing he sees. In order to do something he must establish a closer contact with the beads, something more than just the visual contact. Of course, during the time when the desire for closer contact is building up we can see that his attention wanders; he looks at the beads for a while, then at something else for a while—but the focus of his eyes seems always to return to them.

So he reaches out for this string of beads—and notice how uncoordinated his movements are! He makes a grab in the general direction of the beads, but misses them by a wide margin. He makes one attempt after another, with intervals of wandering attention between attempts, until he finally has the beads clasped within his chubby little fists.

Now he attempts further contact and further manipulation. The beads go into his mouth; they're hard, rather sharp and don't have the taste which he associates with his feedings. So he tries other ways of manipulating—or, to use a more common expression, playing with—this new-found object. He shakes them and listens to the clicking noise they make as they touch. Notice again that his co-ordination is still open to improvement; the beads are in his right hand, and as he waves his right arm up and down, he also moves his left arm, although there is no connection between it and the beads. His motions are still not very economical, in one sense of the word; he makes motions which are not necessary to the manipulation as he is doing it.

But also notice that as he learns he becomes more economical in his motions and more efficient in reaching his goal. When he was learning how to get beads, he used his whole body; he reached for the beads with all his muscles and all his emotions, not just with his right hand and arm. After a while he learns to use only his hand and arm; his focussing is more direct.

This learning process of the infant is surprisingly like the methods which the scientist uses in his laboratory when he is attempting to pry information out of that body of yet-unknown facts we call Nature. We can make this parallelism more clear by putting the baby's actions into words, by assuming that, if the various functions of his body could talk, they would be saying certain things.

Baby's eyes: I see the heads.

Total baby: I want the beads.

Baby's muscles: I am reaching out for the beads.

Baby's eyes: My right arm is going in the wrong direction—
the beads are over there.
Baby's muscles: I'll correct the error; is that better?
Baby's eyes: Yes, but I'm still not going in quite the right
direction.
Baby's muscles: I'll go to the right a little more—there.
Now I'm getting closer. I'll open my hand so that I
can grasp them. That's right—I couldn't pick them
up if my hand were clenched into a fist. Now I have
them.

The scientist is able to speak, so we can quote from him
directly. He would express himself this way: "I have made
an observation, and it would be interesting to see what
applications I can make of this new-found fact. I shall start
with a hypothetical explanation, and I shall make some
experiments to prove or disprove the correctness of the
hypothesis. Now I find out that it is not quite correct, so I
will change my explanation. There, that's better—now I
know how this observation relates to previously-known
facts."

Notice the way that each of them arrives at a chosen
goal: there is first the statement of the goal, then an action
taken. It doesn't seem to make much difference how correct the initial action is, so long as it is corrected; by
making a movement toward the goal, then constantly
changing whatever is incorrect about it, the goal is ulti-
mately reached. Or, to put it another way, one makes a
mistake; by correcting the mistake, one gets closer to the
goal; the process is repeated as long as necessary.

This brings up one of the ways in which we, as a society, have created needless problems for ourselves, as individuals: instead of thinking of a mistake as a necessary part of the learning process, we regard it as something to be avoided. We don't like mistakes; we act as if we were afraid to make mistakes.

Have you ever watched a small boy learning how to throw a ball? He makes a lot of mistakes—and he corrects them, too. If he didn't make mistakes, there would be nothing to correct, and he would never learn to throw.

You might also notice his attitude about his mistakes: he's cheerful about them. A wild pitch will cause him to say, "Not so good—I let go of it too fast." A successful throw will make him grin and say, "Boy, I'm really getting good!"

Compare this with an adult, who has been taught that mistakes are bad, dangerous and wrong. Take the case of the woman who wouldn't leave her house; when asked for an explanation of this she would say, "I'm afraid that I'm going to faint if I go out on the street." Maybe she was correct—maybe she would faint if she went outside the front door. And if she did, that would be tremendously embarrassing; it would be a mistake even to run the risk of it. And so, fearful of making an error, she kept herself a prisoner in her own home.

Perhaps you noticed that we used the word "learning" when we talked about the boy and his ball, and we used the word "taught" when we discussed the fear of mistakes. When we say 'taught," we imply that the person did not learn the lesson by his own volition; instead it was a lesson which was forced upon him. The evaluation of mistakes as "bad" certainly seems to be due to teaching, not to learning—and it's often the case that the lessons we're taught are accompanied with pain.

THE MISTAKE AS THE FOUNDATION OF THE INFERIORITY COMPLEX

Perhaps some of you can recall the process of being taught not to make a mistake. Maybe as a child you were playing with something interesting, some possession of one of the big people. In your efforts to find out more about it, you broke it. You learned that grown-ups' playthings were considerably more fragile than your blocks—and there is also a chance that you were punished. In other words, your efforts to learn were rewarded with a spanking—and the association between mistake-making and pain was set up.

In some cases it is not even necessary for actual pain to occur: the threat of pain is often sufficient to alter the child's conduct. If you were told, "Don't do that—you'll hurt yourself!" you certainly weren't encouraged to learn.

We suspect that this business of learning followed by punishment (or threat of punishment) has something to do with the creation of the so-called "inferiority complex." The person who feels constantly inferior to everyone else, who insists that everyone else is superior to him, has been taught to think and feel that way. And what better way could he be taught such a self-deprecating attitude than by being constantly corrected? He tries to do something—and a fond parent says, "No, darling, you're making a mistake—that's wrong. You should do it this way."

The parent is sincerely trying to help—but a constant repetition of such help will also teach the child that he's wrong, that someone else is right. And after a few years of this, the child comes to the conclusion that he's just not very smart, and another case of inferiority begins to bloom.

It is characteristic of the inferiority complex that the person who carries this mental burden is hesitant about taking action. He'd rather sit back and let somebody else do it first—for that is the lesson which he has been taught. By being led to be uncertain about his actions, he grows to fear action. Action, to him, is the equivalent of making a mistake—and he doesn't want to do that.

As an extreme example of this, there was the man who had been put in an institution for the mentally ill, diagnosed as a case of catatonic schizophrenia. He did nothing; he wouldn't move; he wouldn't even attempt to feed himself. He would sit for hours until one of the attendants would move him, and then he would stay in that position until some outside force acted upon him again. This man was fortunate enough to recover, as only too few do who have this sort of psychosis. After he had returned to normal, he told his docetor that he had thought that he was surrounded by an electric field. Being an electrical engineer, this man knew that if one moves a piece of wire or some other conductor of electricity through an electrical field, a current is

35

set up within the wire. This man said that, during his period of insanity, he was mortally certain that if he moved, he would generate a current within himself and thereby be electrocuted. Rather than take an action which might be a mistake, he had reduced his own activities almost to the point of death.

We see other less dramatic examples every day of how people avoid taking action because they might make a mistake. There is the unhappily married woman who refuses to consider divorce because it might be the wrong thing to do. There is the man who won't go to the doctor because he might find out that there's something wrong with him. Their theme-song seems to be, "Don't do anything—it might be a mistake!"

THE MISTAKE AS A BASIS OF THE "GUILT COMPLEX"

In our society, one of the consequences of making a mistake is a feeling of guilt. It's a little difficult to give a good definition of the guilt-feeling, because it is such a confused, disorganized state of mind. The person is not always certain about what he is guilty of—he's just certain he's guilty. On the other hand, maybe he isn't. He vacillates between the two thoughts, and he can get out of his quandary only by admitting his guilt.

Perhaps we can make the subject of guilt a little more understandable if we say that it appears to be a result of being rejected in all ways except the negative. When we see a guilt-ridden adult, we suspect that in his childhood he was made responsible for all his wrong-doings, and was otherwise ignored. He was almost always scolded and punished, almost never praised or encouraged.

He is taught an extremely limited evaluation of himself: whatever he does is wrong, whatever he is is wrong. There doesn't seem to be any alternative.

The lack of alternative gives the guilt-ridden person a compulsive personality structure. He acts as if he couldn't be anything else besides wrong: whatever good happens as a result of his actions occurs only because he planned something bad—at least, that's what he says. He admits freely that he was going to do something "bad," and the good results were purely coincidental.

Another part of this feeling of being constantly guilty is the urge to confess—and this can easily be carried to an illogical extreme, as in the case of Alfred.

Alfred was a quiet, mousey little man. In spite of having had a high-school education, the jobs he had held were of the most menial sort. He had no vices—and no ambition, either.

His only claim to fame was that he had once confessed to have committed a notorious crime: he claimed to have been responsible for the burning of a home for the feeble-minded, in which twenty of the inmates lost their lives. It took only a superficial investigation for the police to determine that he couldn't possibly have done the deed—and, of course, they were exceedingly annoyed at him.

Several times after this Alfred tried to confess to other crimes, but the police were suspicious of these "confessions" of his and paid very little attention to his claims of guilt.

Finally one of the police officers recognized that these fantasy-crimes, if ignored, might some day lead to an actual crime; through his efforts Alfred was given psychotherapy.

It was found that Alfred had been an illegitimate child; he had been brought up by his mother's parents, who had regarded him as the important factor in his mother's "downfall." They resented having to take care of him, and were strict in their demands for "good behavior." Any deviation from their rules would result in his being told that he was wrong, that he had been born wrong and would never be right, that his mother was no good, and that he was just like his mother.

The grandparents had both died during Alfred's last year in high-school. He went to work and continued with a succession of jobs which demanded a minimum of responsibility. He had no friends; he never dissipated, and he had had no sexual experience with women. Considerably later in his therapy it came out that his only form of sexual expression was masturbation, which was accompanied by fantasies of rape, sodomy, bestiality and other criminal acts.

What was Alfred trying to do when he confessed to a crime which he hadn't committed? We can disregard the reason which he gave the police: "It just seemed like I had to do it." We suggest that the only way Alfred (and any other guilt-ridden person) could get the attention, the love and the contact which he needed (as we all do) was to confess. He had never had the chance to learn that there are other ways to make contact.

Confession is a useful and helpful device, as has been

demonstrated in various societies and by certain religions. As they mean it to be used, confession is a method of learning: the person reviews his past actions, considers them and is helped to think about correcting his behavior.

But this is not what happens in the guilt-complex; in this confession is used for its own sake—not as a learning process. The guilty person continues to do the things which require a confession, in order to have something to be guilty about, so that he can confess it.

We feel that guilt is not necessary. Too many parents treat their children as if they were only capable of evil and error. Children need to be encouraged, need to be praised for their accomplishments as well as being corrected for their mistakes. If there is no reward and only censure, how else can a child feel but guilty?

Encouragement is important to all of us because it is a means by which we learn self-recognition and self-awareness. It is essential for a person to be able to recognize himself as a person, to feel important and capable. And it is an important step toward this self-recognition to be free both to make mistakes and to correct them.

HOW TO MAKE THE MOST OF OUR MISTAKES

It's a strange and unfortunate situation, when you stop to think about it, that some people act as if their only choice were between guilt and inaction. If these people do something, they feel that they've done wrong. What can we do to help them?

We feel that with a change of attitude, a change which

we can all make, we can avoid both inaction and guilt. We can do it by re-considering our attitude toward making mistakes. Consider that a mistake is a method of learning, one of the necessary steps in developing knowledge, that we couldn't learn unless we made mistakes—and what happens to fear of action and to regret over having taken action?

We might say that fear and guilt would disappear—but that wouldn't be quite accurate. It would be better to say that the first step toward correcting these feelings had been taken.

You might take this step by recalling one of your mistakes—then think about it, not as a mistake but as an action, an action that had a purpose. Perhaps you didn't accomplish your purpose by that action—but wasn't it necessary to find out that you couldn't reach your goal by that route?

If you want to be a little more definite about this, we suggest that you take a paper and pencil and jot down your thoughts about this mistake. Make a list of the consequences of making that particular mistake: what were the disadvantages? What were the advantages?

Next—and this is even more important than the preceding step—make another list, but this time consider that your action was *not* a mistake, but something which you deliberately chose to do. Now what are the advantages and disadvantages?

It is interesting to note that when a person does this, he is apt to find that he made the mistake deliberately. We often use this observation in therapy, and find it helpful in increasing the patient's self-understanding.

Take the case of the woman who berated herself because, as she expressed it, she was always annoying her husband. "I know that I make him mad when I say those things to him, but I just can't help myself. The words just seem to come out, and I can't stop them."

By considering her impulsive words, not as a mistake, but as a deliberate action, she came to the conclusion that she was acting as if she *wanted* to make her husband angry with her. The question "Why?" could then be asked—and an answer to it could be found. She was then able to use an alternative approach—one which would not have been possible as long as the action was compulsive.

Supposing that you make a habitual mistake, such as playing the wrong succession of notes on the piano, or always lifting your head in the middle of your golf stroke, of writing "thier" instead of "their." If you do, there is a simple device by which you can change this mistake-making pattern. If you make the mistake deliberately; if you play those notes incorrectly with full intention of doing so; if you make your swing at the ball and voluntarily raise your head in the middle of the stroke; if you will write "thier" a few times and feel the succession of actions which incur in misspelling that word—the chances are that you will no longer be troubled by that mistake.

We might explain the experiment this way: there seems to be a need for taking a certain kind of action which we label as a "mistake"; so long as we repress that action, so long as we are not aware of that need, it comes out involuntarily and undesirably. When we fulfill that need by performing the action because we want to, the need for doing things in that way seems to disappear.

Later on, as you will see, you will find out why you have such needs. The first step, however, is to recognize that you have them, that there is a desire for doing something in a certain way.

This brings us to the next question: why should you want to make a mistake? You can continue your experiment in deliberate error by increasing your awareness of what is going on during the process of mistake-making. Are you ashamed of yourself? Do you become angry? Do you "give yourself hell"? What happens to the various bodily functions when you make a mistake: do you become tense? Does your pattern of breathing change? Do you have any sensations for which there is no present-time stimulus?

Try this experiment and see what happens. You may be surprised.

CHAPTER IV

THE BODY IS PART OF THE MIND

THE CHARACTER PATTERN OF ANXIETY AND NERVOUS TEN-
SION · ORIGINS OF ANXIETY · THE PURPOSE OF ANXIETY · HOW
TO MAKE THE MOST OF ANXIETY

In recent years there has been too much confusion introduced into the picture of living by attempting to define
many of our functions as being purely mental or purely
physical. In many instances this procedure has become
rather ridiculous. The popular magazines have lampooned
the proponents of both schools in cartoons. One shows a
patient reclining on a couch in a psychiatrist's office. The
caption is, "Don't worry. It's all in your body!" The opposite extreme depicts the patient who is obviously in great
physical distress being told reassuringly, "It's all your imagination."

Whether the body is part of the mind or vice versa is not very important; that they affect one another is. Your heart beats and your blood flows without your telling it to. You don't have to tell yourself how to put your feet down when you walk. As a matter of fact, too deliberate attention is apt to make you falter and function less efficiently. But this does not mean that when you are walking, you do not "know" you are walking. Of course you do—the knowledge is in your body, and your mind is also taking account of the activity. The same holds true for every function you participate in. Body knowledge is important.

Why it works this way we shall not attempt to answer. Many explanations have been offered, and you can take your choice of whichever appeals most to you: God, universal law, natural laws, etc. This is not our province. However, we have observed that when we can learn more about how things work, if not why they work that way, this knowledge is applicable and also beneficial.

Let's for the time being accept the point of view that the mind is not separate from the body or independent of it. We have ample evidence that when there is an attempt to emphasize one or the other, something occurs in the human being which is identified as anxiety or unreasonable fear. Nervous tension is the accompanying symptom of anxiety; therefore, when we refer to anxiety, the condition of nervous tension is included.

Let us examine the condition called anxiety, how it works, when it works, etc. Maybe by so doing we can understand it better and can handle it rather than be victims of it. First, let's try to define it. The psychologists, medical doctors and physiologists all agree on this one. It appears to be a state of chronic emergency against a threat (real or imagined), where the individual is so confused and afraid as to what action to take that too little or no action is taken. The sword of Damocles hanging overhead is a good example. We all have experienced some form of anxiety, major or minor, in our lifetime, where we just didn't know what to do and we were afraid to do anything since it might be the wrong thing. It's a very uncomfortable way to feel, and if we remember back to that time, it will be seen that relief came when we performed some sort of action—even if it was running away. Of course, running away is not the best way to handle anxiety, nor is it the only way. We are citing it only to demonstrate an action which is better than staying in an anxious situation to the point where you fall apart from tension. Later in this chapter we shall go into greater detail as to how to handle anxiety. At present we are more concerned with how it works.

There are most likely many conditions present in any state of anxiety that we don't know anything about. Many factors contribute to its general pattern. However, we have identified four of them which, if recognized and worked with, can help greatly in breaking down the terrible grip that anxiety can have over us. They are: Threat—Confusion—Terror—Inactivity. These are not presented separately but in combination. They exist together in every observable case of anxiety. Each factor by itself does not have to pro-

45

duce anxiety, but in combination they almost invariably do.

Let's take, for example, two soldiers going into battle for the first time. Both are in terror and confusion as to the threat they are facing. One just refuses to go on and falls to the ground in a state of paralysis. The other goes on into the battle in spite of his terror and out of the action finds out what the battle is like. He may be hurt, but he has overcome his fear of fear to the point where in the future he is capable of taking some reasonable action in an emergency situation. On the other hand, the soldier who has fallen to the ground in a state of paralysis does not in any way escape the threat presented by the battle, and even if he lives, he may be a psychological cripple for the rest of his life. If all humans behaved as he did in cases of emergency which occur daily in the lives of people, there would soon be an end to the human race.

We have selected an extreme case in the example of the two soldiers. This has been done intentionally because, in the opinion of this author, too much stress has been laid on the imaginary character of any anxiety, rather than on the realness of the threat to the person. To the anxious person the impending result, following a felt threat, is as real as anything that exists in this world. He resents, and properly so, the idea that he is a fool and the insistence that what he is afraid of has no existence. To him it is very real and dangerous. The fact that it may not be real to us doesn't in any way negate his information. It has been observed many times in psychotherapy that when the fear of some act in relation to an "impending" threat is recognized by the therapist as real the patient tackles the problem more vigorously and is capable then of making the necessary revisions. But the revisions are *his*, developing out of *his* sense of reality, based upon *his* contact with the problem.

Threat in itself has both a real and an unreal character. Its real meaning is in how it is reacted to. Threat is not a complete action but a stimulus for action. For example: a man may point a gun at you. This would be considered real threat. However, the gun may not be loaded. Also, the man may have no intention of hurting you at all; it may be an experiment to test something or other. Then, on the other hand, the gun may be loaded and the intention of the gunman is that of murder. These facts are not known until the complete action is unfolded. People have been known to drop dead from fright at the mere pointing of a toy pistol at them. Is their death unreal? Was the fright unreal? Similarly, men have been killed because they mistook a real gunman with intentions of murder for a prankster. This discussion is not meant to be a lesson on how to react to a gun pointed at you, but as an illustration of the different aspects of "reality."

The threat of war is real. We didn't use the example merely to prove a point. Most anxieties develop out of situations of real threat as serious as war—fear of starvation, fear of the loss of loved ones, fear of death, etc. If the threats that confront the anxious person were purely imaginary, the condition of anxiety would be relatively easy

47

to deal with. However, anxiety is a very strong emotional state. It is true that there are many distortions present, but for it to have become so strong and pervasive, it must have originally been based on a very real threat.

Another example of anxiety at work can be seen in the case of two men eating the same food in a new restaurant. Neither of them knows what the food is going to be like, but they are hungry and so they begin to eat. One chews his food well and finds the savor; the other toys with the food, lightly mouthing and rejecting it. At the end of the meal, the one who gave in to the experience by really eating the food feels very good and is no longer hungry. On the other hand, his companion is sick both from hunger and the nausea which he introduced into the picture. He blames the food, although it didn't affect his companion. So he finds another reason: his stomach is sensitive and he must be careful. But what does it add up to? Each time he approaches a new food in a new situation he has prepared the ground for the next illness which goes with new food. Eventually, if this pattern is not broken, he will begin to feel the same way about all food, even the food he is familiar with, since he will project strange, dangerous qualities into that, too.

What are we driving at in giving these examples? We are trying to illustrate that we can only learn and continue to live healthily out of the experiences which we really participate in. There is no solution in attempting to avoid danger in a situation by doing nothing. Doing nothing is antithetical to life itself. In an organism that is geared to living, doing nothing produces a state of tension that will lead to the perfect doing-nothing state known as death.

Is the anxious person trying to die? No, we reject that theory. He is trying to live, but somehow he has confused continued living with the avoidance of activity. When he can understand how such a confusion developed, he can snap out of it, since he really doesn't want to die.

Fear can be viewed in two different ways: one, as terror—hopelesness—death; two, as excitement—something to be learned—continued living. Out of fear we can learn many things which aid in the more enjoyable life. Out of the fear of darkness man discovered light and was able to explore the darkness and use what was there. Out of the fear of his enemies, man discovered weapons with which to repel them. Out of the fear of hunger, man discovered agriculture and husbandry. The list is virtually endless. Fear can lead to the investigation of the unknown, with trials and tribulations it is true, but also with great rewards.

On the other hand, fear can be viewed as an insurmountable obstacle, leading to more and more pain and finally to apathy and death. The latter version of fear is anxiety. Can we overcome the pattern? Is it a necessary pattern for continued living? Is it an integral part of human existence? Anxiety can be overcome. It is not necessary for living and it is not an integral part of human existence. It is behavior that has been learned incorrectly and, if it has been learned, it can also be unlearned.

Since the beginning of time, man has successfully negotiated many challenges out of the vast unknown of life. Today he is better equipped than before to overcome any of the difficulties which may beset him. The same processes he discovered to overcome the difficulties of the past are available to him today with many new additions. Step one is to identify the enemy (it's very tough trying to fight a shadow). Step two is to give battle, since it is only out of direct contact that any lesson can be learned. Step three is to synthesize the new knowledge so that it can be employed to fight future threats.

Fear cannot be abolished. It can be viewed as challenge, an integral part of the living process, and as such *can be used productively.*

ORIGINS OF ANXIETY

Of the many theories presented on this subject by the different schools of psychology and their fore-runners, we prefer the synthesis developed out of the original observations of Sigmund Freud.

Anxiety seems to originate out of serious threat experienced by the person at a time when he was capable of reacting to this threat in only one way—trembling and limited activity. Such a condition existed in all of us when we were infants or quite young children and we were surrounded by things and forces that were so much bigger and stronger than we were. At that time our ability to identify forces and objects was first being discovered by us. Under those circumstances how else could we react to threat? We could cry. But in many instances crying was punished by spanking. The ability to move and to fight back was relatively undeveloped. All too frequently any such expression was beaten down by the powerful adults and thus these experiences only added to the fear. Similarly the experiences of contact of different kinds had not yet taken place, so that we had no other frame of reference for what was happening, other than to view each new disturbing experience as a threat.

The growing child observed that there were times when something of a disturbing and threatening nature was present, he would tremble and become relatively inactive. Eventually, the threat and disturbance would pass. Is it too hard to conjecture that this could be equated by the infant as a way to deal with threat and disturbance? Is it too far-fetched to assume that when new and disturbing factors entered his field of contact, he should rely on a pattern of behavior that had previously been successful?

Yet, when we observe the growing child, he does seem to act in the manner described. Until he discovers a better method of coping with the distressing situations he encounters in life, he continues to react this way to most "threats" even when he has accomplished the adult state and is capable of strength, mobility and thought.

In a great many fields of action he does learn how to re-evaluate and adjust his behavior to the job at hand, which is why he reaches the adult stage. However, it does seem that in the areas where anxiety exists he is still relying on a first-learned pattern of trembling and inactivity. The areas may be of slight or greater importance. They range from anxieties about food, climate, traveling, height, special sounds, closeness, fear of the strange, etc. to the more serious ones such as sex, inferiority, economic insecurity, persecution, etc.

Freud observed that in psychotherapy the anxious person could be directed in recalling a great deal about the "origin" of this destructive pattern of behavior. In so doing the patient could make a comparison between the rigid type of behavior and the more elastic and efficient behavior which he exercised in the successful areas of his life. And eventually this realization could lead to the discharging of the previously compelled allegiance to trembling and inactivity as a way to respond to threatening situations, and a new and more beneficial type of behavior could be learned. Most modern psychotherapy is based on this approach, regardless of what name the school bears. No matter what emphasis it verbally announces, the goal is to eliminate the present confusion from which the patient suffers as the result of earlier threatening experiences improperly understood.

THE PURPOSE OF ANXIETY

To find anything that could even be called a reasonable purpose for anxiety, it is necessary to enter the field of pure speculation. The evidence available in terms of what we know of human behavior leads us to the belief that in the human being anxiety is a function that is totally destructive.

Any attempt at finding a basis for its existence at all

seems to be limited to the study of similar states in the lower animals. It has been observed that dogs and cats and other domesticated animals display symptoms that are very similar to what is called anxiety when they are restricted and punished for indulging in their natural interests. But when they are not subjected to these impositions of human restraint, these symptoms are not evident. Animals used in psychological experiments showed anxiety-like states when they were subjected to pain in situations that they couldn't understand or overcome. However, in their natural state and surroundings they do not seem to manifest anything that approximates anxiety.

The opossum playing dead when it is in a situation of danger seems to display a reaction that bears a remote resemblance to human anxiety, except that for the opossum it's been proven a good survival method, since most animals will not eat what they have not killed. However, when the emergency is over the opossum goes about its natural business normally.

In the rabbit whose main defense against attack is flight, the using of this immobile type of reaction to threat certainly doesn't work out well, especially in these modern times when we see him "freeze" in front of an oncoming automobile and get flattened into the road.

The closest we can come to finding a condition that resembles anxiety as expressed in humans is in the behavior of the very young and helpless birds and animals. This occurs before they have developed the strength and mobility to either fight back, run, or fly away. These creatures are

53

quiet and motionless, except for trembling, when strange animals are in the vicinity. In such instances being motionless and quiet is necessary and valuable in terms of survival, since noise and movement could attract the strange animals to the young and helpless ones and they might wind up as food, prematurely. However, it has been observed that when these young animals and birds arrive at maturity of strength and mobility, this mechanism is seldom if ever again employed.

The examples given and many others which we shall not list (since this information is available in existing literature for the more serious student) have led us to the following. At one time anxiety (by which we mean a situation of fear coupled with inactivity) or something like it may have had a purpose. In times of threat when we were capable of no other defense, it was best for us to sort of "play dead" to deceive the threatening enemy. By so doing it appeared as if we had a better chance for remaining alive until we could develop better means of protection. But today, when we are grown and strong and have weapons and skills and the thinking capacity to overcome practically any threat, anxiety is a useless and harmful sort of behavior. The sooner we stop relying on it as a method for getting us out of difficult situations, the sooner will it go into ancient history, where it most likely belongs. There seems to be very little point in getting ourselves all tense and prepared for action in terms of a projected threat and remaining in that tense state without taking any kind of action until we fall apart from the shaking.

HOW TO MAKE THE MOST OF ANXIETY

As you can guess from what you have read in the previous sections on anxiety, we believe that you can make the most of your anxieties by not having them. Whether the anxiety is related to the sex problem, family problem, economic problem, study problem, health problem, or the anticipation of some future threat, you will be better able to work out the problem by dispensing with the anxiety.

The first step in the elimination of anxiety requires one's taking an action which is related to the problem at hand. If the action is not the right one, it can be corrected and another action undertaken. But you really can't tell much without trying first. If one doesn't undertake an action in relation to a problem and just thinks about it, the problem grows bigger and bigger. Soon the process of thinking is no longer thinking; it is worrying, and *that* is anxiety.

How will you recognize whether you are anxious or not? This question is not as silly as it sounds. You've seen cartoons of a man mad with rage, breaking dishes and yelling at his wife, "What do you mean saying I'm angry?" The anxious person many times feels this way about his behavior. He feels there is nothing wrong with it and that it is logical.

George, a clinic patient, starting out this way: "I'm not anxious or afraid." With a quivering voice and a trembling body, he said, "Any normal person would act the same way as I do in this sort of a fix."

What was the "fix?" It turned out that George needed

55

more money than he was earning at his job. It was getting more and more difficult for his wife to make ends meet and keep the two kids in clothes and food on his small salary. He was afraid to ask the boss for a raise in spite of the fact that business was good and he was underpaid. He was afraid that if he did ask for a raise, he would be fired and then he might not get another job, and since he had very little reserve cash, his family would starve, and the landlord would dispossess them, and what would the neighbors say, and he came from such a good family it would hurt their pride, and he was so ashamed. This all poured forth from George in a flood and a rising crescendo. He worked himself up into a terrific pitch of tension, which wound up in his breaking down into hysterical crying.

After he had quieted down he was asked if his boss had been known to fire anyone who asked for a raise in salary. He answered, "No." And why did he feel that he wouldn't get another job in the event he lost this one? "I don't know," he answered. "I just feel that way." To the question of whether he was good at his work, he said, "I am very good. I was tops at school and in all my years in business I have never heard a complaint. And yet I feel very uncertain of how my employer feels about this."

It was then suggested that on the morrow he ask his employer for the increase in salary. He would be as calm as possible about it, but he would raise the question. If this didn't work, then another course of action would be considered. It was quite obvious even to George that his present state of tension was as bad as anything else could possibly be, and this would have to be tried.

It so happened that George did get his raise and, as a matter of fact, was told by his employer that he was pleased that George had introduced the subject. He had recognized George as a very good worker, but every time he found himself in contact with George, George had acted so nervously that he had avoided bringing it up himself. He felt that from this point on George and he could have a more understanding relationship. Of course, all of George's anxieties didn't disappear with this one action, but it was a very good start.

A case quite similar was that of Joyce. Her problem as she stated it was that she had no boy friends. She was young, age 25, pretty, dressed well and was quite intelligent, but had no boy friends. Did she like boys? Yes, of course, but that wasn't right, was it? She was afraid that they knew she liked them and laughed at her because she was improper and foolish. Did she know any boys? Oh, yes, she worked with many, and her brothers' friends would call at the house, but she would have nothing much to say or do with them, because they laughed at her. Did any of them ever ask her to go out with them on a date? Oh, yes, but she wouldn't go because they really didn't mean it. How did she know? Oh, she just felt that way. When she was fifteen years old, her mother had punished her for permitting one of the boys at school to walk her home. Her mother had said that she was much too young for that sort of stuff, that people would laugh at her, even the boys would laugh at her for trying to act so grown-up. She remembered that her mother had always disapproved of her being friendly with the boys in the neighborhood even when she was younger. However, here was a funny twist. When she was twenty-one her mother began to scold her for not having any dates with boys. "Did she want to be an old maid?" And she had been bothering her this way up until the present. Joyce couldn't believe her mother meant what she was saying, and she was very afraid of doing anything about it.

Joyce was asked whether for the sake of an experiment she would go out with one of the boys and try to have a good time and come back to the doctor and tell him all about it. She consented only when she was convinced that the doctor thought she should and was sure there was nothing wrong in her doing this.

Joyce went out on her first grown-up date and she had a very good time. Of course, she was a bit tense about it at the beginning, but as the evening went on her tension diminished. After that first date, she had many more, some with the same boy and some with other boys. Some of the dates were more pleasant than the others, but out of all these experiences Joyce was able to discover what it was she wanted and enjoyed most in her relations with men. Today Joyce is happily married, and although she is not completely anxiety free, she has learned that there is a way to cope with anxiety. And she is prepared to use this way at any time.

Of course, there was a lot more to these two cases than

has been mentioned here. What has been stressed has been the importance of taking a related action to deal with an unquestionable need of the person. There are many other aspects of anxiety that must be considered such as the fear of failure and shame and guilt. Yet what better way is there to begin this attack on those enemies than the taking of an action that smokes them out of hiding where we can see them for what they are? Can the fear of failure be defeated in any more effective way than by a successful action? And doesn't shame become just another word when it is compared with the result of actions that have produced health, well-being and life? And doesn't guilt become like a toy whip used to intimidate children when we have an adult frame of reference born out of adult actions and functions?

A study of man and his history has led us to the following conclusion: it appears as though we do things because there is a real need for something, and then we appraise what we have obtained and the method by which we have accomplished it. When we lose sight of the necessary action behind any need, and attempt to formulate a practice of thought without action, we lay the basis for our becoming the victims of processes which must go on whether we acknowledge them in our thinking or not. The result of such an attempt leads to anxiety, the failure to acknowledge the need for continued activity and function.

Anxiety tries to use the mental function alone to solve the problems that rise out of body needs. This can't be done. The body needs more than "thoughts" to feed it, and the mind needs more than abstract mental function to keep it healthy. There can't be a separation, no matter how we may try to accomplish it. Anxiety succeeds in accomplishing only one thing, the eventual destruction of both mind and body.

Man learned to make clothes for himself because he was cold, to acquire food because he was hungry, to deal with his enemies because he wanted to continue living. First there was need and then action and the modifications to promote better survival.

Which way shall we choose? Shall we choose action, inspired by need, backed up by a history of successful thinking? Or shall it be "thinking" in terms of fear only, with no action to determine whether the thinking is right or not? You are the best judge of whether you are anxious and worried and full of nervous tension. You can tell because you are doing less, getting less and are much less comfortable. You know whether you're angry at everybody though you may be afraid to show it. You can feel whether you're afraid of everything and predict that it will be worse. You know the symptoms. We all know the symptoms. The only answer to this condition is action. Not just any action, but related action in terms of what is bothering you. In illness like this, when you see the doctor, only you can help the doctor. In the final analysis of anxiety, YOU ARE THE DOCTOR!

CHAPTER V

THE SEXUAL SIDE OF THE PICTURE

WHY IMPOTENCE? · WHY FRIGIDITY? · WHY HOMOSEXUAL-
ITY? · HOW TO MAKE THE MOST OF SEX

LET's start our discussion of sex by agreeing that sex is real,
that it is important, and that without it life could not
continue.

Next, let us try to understand that our knowledge of sex
includes a lot of ideas which are *not* sex. In our present-day
way of living, we have imposed a great many moral concepts on the expression of sex, thereby creating a marked
confusion between sex itself and our concept of sex. To
make a comparison, we could say that we have an action
called sex, and we also have a picture of what that activity
"should" be—and there is confusion between the actuality
and the picture.

61

Let us consider that sex is a powerful real force, a force which keeps our race alive and gives us a reason for living. Imposed on this force are ideas—ideas which can change the direction of the force but cannot destroy it. The force continues to be what it is regardless of what forms of expression are permitted or denied.

We can also recognize that any force which is as real and powerful as the sex-force can take many forms and can appear as a part of many other activities. No matter what form our sex-force—or life-force—takes, it still exists, powerful and pleasurable.

We want to emphasize that word *pleasurable*. We feel that any activity which is so closely connected with the very production of life must have an element of pleasure in it. Denial of the pleasures of living is an absurd distortion of fact.

As Aristotle, the famous Greek philosopher, once said, "And whatsoever is in conformity with nature is pleasant and all creatures pursue pleasure in keeping with their nature."

The reason for the emphasis on the pleasures of living and the pleasures of the sexual side of living is that there seems to be confusion about it. A great many people seem to take the opposite viewpoint, saying that life is all sorrow and travail and that the expression of life through sexual pleasure is evil.

And yet we notice that, while they *say* that sex is evil, they don't *act* as if it were. The people who insist that sex is nasty still seek sexual pleasure; their seeking is consistent, even though it may be surreptitious and disguised.

We have observed that when the sexual aspects of human behavior are approached more realistically, people begin to feel better and can experience more happiness. That is the attitude which we'll try to maintain in this book—to look at sex as a natural function, rather than as a moral problem. After all, the doctor is concerned with health and happiness, not morality; moral problems seem to be the concern of other groups which have their own special axes to grind.

In the absence of a realistic, naturalistic attitude towards sex, we see confusion. As a result of the confusion we see fear. Sex, instead of being pleasurable, becomes fearsome and terrifying.

The fear of sex, or of some of the aspects of sex, seems to be at the root of every sexual disorder. As a result of their fears, some people restrict their sexual expressions, inhibit their sexual responses and direct their sexual outlets into channels which are unhealthy and unhappy. Even these outlets are fearsome—they are merely a lesser fear.

WHY IMPOTENCE?

The impotent male is, characteristically, a fearful male. He is afraid of sex; he regards sex as evil. As a result of his fear, he becomes unable to have sexual relations.

He has other fears, too. He is afraid of himself; he feels inferior, he feels that he is evil, he feels that he is unworthy of the joys of sex. He is even afraid of being impotent, and, as a result, becomes even more impotent.

We should mention that there are other causes of impotency than fear. Once in a while we see someone who, through accidental injury or a congenital absence of parts, is unable to have intercourse. These cases are quite rare, however; most impotent males are structurally normal. It is only their sexual function which is not what it could be.

This is confirmed by the results of psychotherapy: in most cases recovery of the ability to perform the sex act was effected when the fear of "evil" and inferiority was re-examined and re-evaluated in the light of *present feelable stimulus*.

The impotent male, then, does not look any different from you or me. He doesn't necessarily look timid or under-sized or weak; the chances are that the appearance which he presents in public is quite the opposite. He may be quite talkative, active and imaginative; he may talk as if he were extremely sexually active and will, if encouraged, do some bragging about his sexual conquests.

The purpose of this section, however, is not to tell you how to recognize the impotent male. It is, rather, an attempt to help us understand more about ourselves and to help us to do more for ourselves. We all seem to suffer a little from this fear or that fear, and when we are able to see the similarity between ourselves and others, there is less danger of our trying to be something impossible.

A part of the central core of impotence is an impossibly unrealistic idea of the sex act. The impotent male has an idea of sex—and he reacts to his idea more than he does to his actual sensations. He expects sex to fulfill his ideas—

but his ideas were not derived from his own experiences. Instead, his ideas came from what he was taught, from what he was told, rather than from his own sensations. His ideas of the sex act make it so glorious, so wonderful and at the same time so evil, that he asks himself, "How can poor unworthy me accomplish this super-colossal act?"

When the opportunity for sex is presented, then, "poor unworthy me" is incapable of acting in all the different ways in which he imagines he should act. Who could? He has such an exaggerated idea of what sex "should" be—he "should" have a twelve inch penis, he "should" be able to have twenty orgasms, he "should" look like a composite of all the movie heroes. This is impossible, naturally—and so there is conflict within him.

There is further conflict between his ideas of brutal masculinity and his own feelings of tenderness, between his conception of a woman as a goddess and as a harlot. There is conflict, confusion and anxiety. And yet the need to experience the sex act still drives him. What can he do?

As an example of impotency, we present the case of Walter.

Walter was a thirty-seven-year-old man who had always been troubled by impotency. He had tried the usual medical treatments, including the use of male sex hormones and prostatic massage; he had even experimented with the drugs which are supposed to stimulate sex function—all to no avail.

At first glance one would never have suspected that Walter had this sort of trouble. His appearance was definitely masculine; he had a heavy beard and deep voice along with an athletic physique.

He wasn't too happy about coming to the psychosomaticist, but he agreed to do so because his wife, whom he had married one month before, was threatening annulment of their marriage on the grounds of his impotency. He felt that treatment by a doctor who dealt with mental and emotional illnesses was a sign that he was "neurotic" or "crazy," and for the greater part of the first session he was very much on the defensive.

Walter's parents were "fine, respectable, church-going people"; during his years of growing up, they stressed the importance of being "fine," "respectable," and "church-going" and expected him to be the same. They insisted that Walter get good grades in school; if he didn't, he was punished—but if he did, he was not praised.

Sex was a forbidden topic in his family; people who had anything to do with sex were condemned as "dirty, evil, wicked and degenerate." Even the little acts of affection among members of the family were frowned upon; Walter never saw his parents show any demonstration of love for each other, and receiving a kiss or a hug from either of his parents was virtually unknown.

As he grew older Walter attempted at various times to rebel against the rigid discipline which pervaded his family life, but each time he was punished. Punishment usually took the form of being sent to his room, or being deprived of some of his few privileges, though occasionally he would receive what was called "a good, sound whipping."

His sexual development had been quite slow; up until the age of eighteen, when he went to college, he had had no sexual experience other than a few furtive attempts at masturbation. During his college years the only additional sexual activity was peeking through bedroom windows in the hope of seeing a woman undressing. He was almost caught at his "Peeping Tom" activities several times, yet he persisted in spite of his narrow escapes.

After his graduation from college he resumed living with his parents. They persisted in treating him as if he were a boy, not a man, so after a year of resentful unhappiness he moved to an apartment of his own. His parents objected strenuously, but Walter ignored their objections.

With his new freedom and independence he set for himself the goal of having sexual experience with a woman. His drive in this direction was so strong as to be almost obsessive. He soon found, however, that the goal was unattainable, for every time he found a willing female partner he was thwarted by his inability to have an erection.

He read voluminously about sexual aberrations, and became quite an authority on the subject. He also built up a collection of books dealing with the more pornographic aspects of sex, and this, added to his genuine hospitality and good-fellowship, made him quite popular.

His impotency persisted, however, and for this reason he avoided marriage until the age of thirty-seven. At that time he met a girl who was gentle, intelligent and understanding, and he felt that they could make a go of marriage, in spite of his inabilities.

67

It took the doctor several sessions to acquire all this information. He then decided to use an experimental technique; he arranged for an appointment two weeks from that day and gave Walter explicit instructions that he was to continue to sleep with his wife, but that under no circumstances was he to touch her or to attempt any sort of sex play. The doctor insisted that Walter follow these instructions without deviation, and he agreed to do so.

Three days later Walter called the doctor in great consternation. "Doctor, I don't know what you're going to do with me. I tried to follow your instructions, but I just couldn't control myself. I had intercourse with my wife last night."

"Any sign of impotency?" the doctor asked.

"Well, no—but—"

And this is the case of Walter, who didn't succeed in being potent until he was given orders not to touch his wife. What was it that happened to permit him to do what he had never been able to do before? Was it the need to rebel against the doctor's orders? Or was it just a coincidence?

It might be any or all of these reasons. We would also add this explanation: Walter's own sensations were given the chance to grow strong. During the nights when he was lying in bed with his wife, trying not to touch her, he became aware that he had sensations, and that he could feel them grow in intensity. They became so intense that the activity of sex was the logical result.

Previous to this, Walter had not been aware that he had

these sensations. He had been so absorbed in his ideas of sex, in his fears of sex, in the fears of his own impotency, that he didn't get around to feeling the sensations which lead to sexual expression. Focussing his attention on the sensations of sex, instead of the concepts of what he had been told about sex, enabled him to accomplish the sex act.

This is our explanation. We think that it's a good explanation because in the cases we have observed, when an impotent male is guided to the point where he can feel his own sensations, potency is usually the result. Of course, there can be other explanations besides this.

It is interesting to observe how people act toward their own sensations. Have you noticed how some people shake hands? There is the limp, timid handshake that seems to say, "You won't hurt me because I'm so weak." There is the forceful, bone-crushing grip which indicates that the person is going to overwhelm you if he can. In both of these types there is probably a failure in experiencing the actual sensations of a handclasp. These people are more concerned with their own fears than they are with the communication which a handshake can contain.

Are we making a mountain out of a mole-hill? Are we giving more significance to a handshake than it deserves? We don't think so—and here is why: any sort of human contact will produce a sensation, and the ignoring of any one sensation, even so simple a one as a handclasp, leads to the tendency to ignore other sensations.

It is in the simple areas of physical contact that confusions begin. For example, consider the child who loves to kiss and embrace his parents; he is fulfilling his needs for contact-sensation. If he is told not to be so demonstrative, that "it isn't nice," the result is a confusion between his own sensations and what his parents think about his actions. A child who is treated in this way may grow up with compulsion to avoid all contact since it has been identified with "Don't—it's not nice."

Or take the child who loves to play in his warm bath: he enjoys the pleasurable sensations from contact with the warm water. But if some over-zealous adult says, "Hurry up—don't waste so much time—wash your privates but don't handle them," what a confusion that creates! It's very easy for the child to interpret this as meaning that it's bad to enjoy bathing.

If the pleasures of kissing contact aren't "nice," if the enjoyment of bathing contact is "bad," it is all too easy to set up the equation that all personal pleasure should be avoided. What, then, is left?

To the mind of a child the only possibility is to do the proper things—the things which are told to him as being proper. And what are they? According to too many people, the proper things are those which nobody will stop you from doing; if you're doing something and no one tries to prevent you from doing it, then it's proper. If it's not proper, then some sort of prohibition is attached to it.

According to this definition it is proper to be sick, to be unhappy, to restrict contact, to avoid personal pleasure. Does this sound absurd? You might give some thought to this: the things which we are permitted to do, or are urged to do, frequently seem to be unpleasant. The things which we are not permitted to do seem to be pleasant.

To express it another way, there is a tendency in our civilization to classify actions as either forbidden or compulsory. If a thing is proper, then it's compulsory; if it's improper, then it's compulsory to avoid doing it. And whenever there is compulsion, there is also the chance for a psychosomatic disease such as impotency to develop.

What can we do about it? Are we forced to sigh and say, "Well, that's the way it is, and I guess I'd better make the best of it." We don't think that's necessary. There is an action which can be taken, an action which can help us to correct this mistake.

We can begin all over again to learn how really wonderful it is to feel sensations—and to define sensations as good, not evil. The simple act of holding a piece of cloth in the fingers can be enjoyed for the sensation it is. The excitement connected with the taste of food can be enjoyed. We can discover that food can be something more than mere fuel for our bodies—there is a joy in the sensation of chewing our food, a joy which may have been lost because we haven't paid enough attention to it, but which can be rediscovered. In the rediscovery of our own sensations we can find pleasure.

What's wrong with pleasure? It never hurt anyone. True, some things can be overdone—but we have observed that they are overdone only when other areas of pleasure or sensation are denied expression. It is possible to be moderate and temperate when compulsions no longer rule us.

71

The impotent male is a compulsive. He can overcome this by learning how to enjoy his sensations. You can be sure he has the capacity for enjoyment—we all have it. When he can enjoy the touch of the hand, it will lead to the touch of the lips, which will lead to the gentle embrace, which will mingle with the pleasure of the smells, which leads to the stronger embrace—and so on.

Remember that we are not talking about the idea of all this, but the *actual sensations*. Sensations have taught men for millions of years and will continue to do so long after the confusions of our times have become microscopic scratches on the tablets of history.

Before concluding this section, we wish to present another observation: the mutuality of pleasure. It is a wonderful thing to experience—and it comes about when one is equal to feeling his sensations and believing in them. Without this ability, another form of mutuality enters the picture: the mutuality of defensiveness and distrust.

Have you ever noticed, when you are with someone you like, and when you begin to feel good and warm and happy, that the feeling spreads and envelops your partner, too? Have you also observed that when you are with the same person and a situation arises when you begin to question your feelings, your partner can sense this? An experience like the first is joyous—the second can end in tragedy.

Try believing in yourself and your feelings. Instead of talking yourself up or down, try finding out what you are.

We close this section on the impotent male by mentioning that there are other ways in which impotence can be manifested: sadism and satyriasis.

By sadism we refer to the condition wherein the man's sexual enjoyment seems to depend upon the amount of pain which he can inflict on his partner. He seems to act as if he *must* inflict pain in order to prove himself to be a man. Obviously, this is another version of the case given previously, where impotence is a result of fear; the impotent male shows his fear by giving up his sexual powers, while the sadist shows his fear of women by acting as if they were enemies who had to be beaten into submission.

Satyriasis is the name applied to the condition of the insatiable male—the man who acts as if he had to have intercourse with every woman. He, too, is afraid of sex; his fear is such that he must have constant reassurance. He tries to reassure himself of his own potency by having intercourse repeatedly—but the fear remains in spite of his over-activity.

In this condition it is probable that the man is not in contact with his partner, that he is not aware of the sensations which he is getting from the sex act. At any rate, our observations show us that when he does become aware of his own sensations, his obsession disappears and his contacts with women become more moderate and more pleasurable and satisfying.

WHY FRIGIDITY?

Frigidity, the condition in which a woman doesn't like sex, exists in many forms. In every form of this all too common complaint, however, there is one common factor: fear of men.

The frigid woman seldom recognizes that she has such a fear. If it is suggested that she might be afraid of men, she usually says, "Afraid of a mere man? That's ridiculous! They're just like children—stupid and insensitive. I've yet to meet the man whom I can't beat at his own game."

Some frigid women say they hate sex; some say they find it mildly enjoyable, but never have an orgasm; some frigid women say that sex is wonderful and that they can never get enough of it.

It may seem strange to call these three different types by the same term of "frigid"—but this apparent contradiction becomes clear when we say that a frigid woman is one who is afraid.

In a book such as this, where only one chapter is given over to the sexual side of the picture, it would be impossible to go into great detail about the complexities of frigidity. We believe that you can get a better understanding of the problem if we use some case histories rather than do a lot of theorizing.

We shall talk about two types of frigidity: the first, a woman who didn't enjoy sex relations, in spite of the fact that she was married and the mother of children; the second case will be that of a woman who chased men in order to be with them, but still wasn't satisfied.

Anne was an attractive woman in her middle thirties. On the surface she seemed to be one of those fortunate people who have everything. Her husband was handsome, successful and devoted; she had two fine sons; her home was comfortable and pleasant and she had no economic problems.

It seemed as if Anne had everything which could make a woman happy—but behind her conventionally happy exterior was a worried, fearful and resentful woman. She hated her husband, resented her two boys and felt that she was neither a wife nor a mother. She didn't want to be married, and yet she didn't want a divorce. As she expressed it, "I just go on, day in and day out, making life a kind of hell for my family. They'd be better off if I were dead."

The chief reason for her coming to the doctor was that she had been having fantasies about killing her husband or her sons or all three of them. She would start to daydream, then suddenly realize that she was having visions of herself as a murderess; she became worried about these recurring ideas and sought help.

All this came out in the first visit or so. In digging a little deeper in Anne's attitude towards males in general, the doctor soon discovered that she had never experienced an orgasm.

"I think I know what 'an orgasm' means—I've heard the other girls talk about it—but I've never experienced anything like that."

There were a few occasions, she said, when she had attempted sexual relations with men other than her husband—but this, too, was a disappointment. There was no difference between an affair with one man or one with another. With each of these extra-marital relationships there was the fear that she couldn't really satisfy the man.

75

She didn't bother to try to satisfy her husband. "I don't have to—he's so interested in his own pleasure that it's all over before I even have a chance to get started. Oh, I let him take me, of course, but I'm always glad when it's all over."

In considering her early sexual experiences, Anne told how she first started to masturbate at the age of ten. Shortly thereafter her mother caught her in the act and punished her with a beating; this was followed by a "heart to heart" talk about the evils of sex, the ingratitude of men and the horrors that awaited any girl who enjoyed men. Since that time, she said, every time she masturbated she would feel compelled to stop before the climax because of a strange dread of discovery and horrible punishment.

Anne also told the doctor about her two older brothers; they teased and tortured and plagued her all during childhood, yet whenever she complained to her mother about this, she would be scolded for provoking these disagreements. Her father, too, favored the boys; there were fishing trips and camping trips for them, but Anne wasn't invited —such expeditions weren't for girls.

"I hated them—they got all the fun and I didn't have any."

After Anne's marriage at the age of nineteen she grew out of that feeling toward her brothers; she saw them frequently and even enjoyed their company.

Toward her mother Anne always felt very strangely; she viewed her as a cold, hateful woman—but still she was dependent on her and wanted to please her. Every time her mother disagreed with what she was doing or planning,

Anne felt very disturbed and would give in to her mother's wishes in order to attain relief from this disturbance.

Anne's father had died shortly after her marriage; she said that she felt relieved rather than sorrowful at his death. She couldn't remember ever having loved him—as a matter of fact when she was a child, she hated him because he excluded her and favored her brothers.

As she talked about her relationships with her father and her brothers, Anne began to recognize certain similarities between them and her husband. All of them were older than she was; they all kept her from doing some of the things she wanted to do and made her do things that she didn't want to. They had interests from which she was excluded; they caused her pain. It wasn't fair!

In the discussion of her present problem, Anne said that she always submitted to her husband's sex demands, which averaged about three times a week. "He's never satisfied, though—one night he slapped me and told me I was a lump of clay, not a woman." With this she burst into tears and moaned, "What do men want of me? What can I do?"

Fortunately for this woman, psychotherapy was able to help her. From the beginning of her sessions there was a progressive improvement. After three months the strain went out of her to the degree that her feelings toward her husband became those of a more normal woman. The sex act was no longer a threat—instead it was becoming a pleasure. It felt good to participate—to feel—to be a part of a married couple, instead of a lonely individual, present in the flesh yet not participating.

She also found that she was able to disagree with her husband without the disagreement's having to be the whole picture, without feeling it necessary to hate him because of a disagreement. It was possible to agree with him, too, without the necessity of viewing him as a god, or the most wonderful person in the world.

The hate was turning into understanding. She was beginning to see him as a person, like herself, having both inadequacies and capabilities. She could look at her children in a more realistic way: she could get angry at them for some of the things they did without having to feel guilty about not being a good mother. They became a real part of her life, not a threat, and she became able to reach out and give them the necessary warm, feminine love which every mother has to give.

How did this come about? What was it in therapy that enabled her to make these changes? For one thing, when she was able to recognize that she was afraid of men, it was easier for her to see why she feared them. In her childhood, men had "prevented" her from getting the things she needed. The warmth she needed from her mother was "taken" by her father. She had been neglected and her brothers favored. The right to experience and express her own sensations had been denied her.

As a result, in order to survive she had rejected and denied her own sensations. But this is an impossibility, for sensations can't be denied; they can only be repressed or changed.

She had changed her feelings into a hatred of men. With

hate there is fear, and so she had been afraid. Each time she had had contact with men, the fear and hatred loomed so large that her other sensations could not be felt.

When she began to realize all this, she began to look at her husband with new feelings. She saw him as a man—not her father, not her brothers, not the threat with which her mother used to frighten her—but *her* man, warm to sleep with, a good companion, satisfying to live with.

That was the case of Anne—a woman who seemed to hate sex. Here's another case—a woman who also hated sex but who concealed her hatred in abnormal sexual activity.

Sally was a flat-chested, under-weight girl in her late twenties when she came in for psychotherapy. Her skin was muddy, and there was a tenseness about her that reminded the doctor of a drug addict in need of a "shot." She did not look at the doctor; instead her gaze wandered about the room. She seemed unable to keep on any one subject—and yet her intellect was superior to normal.

Her story came out with a queer mixture of defiance and apology. She was getting ready to commit suicide, she said. And why?

"You'll probably think I'm awful," she answered, "but the only pleasure I have in life is having intercourse—and, frankly, it's getting harder and harder for me to find men."

She told of her search for partners, how it had grown more frantic and less satisfactory. She hinted that she had even tried to "pick up" drunks at bars—but they weren't much good. She had even tried women, but they weren't satisfactory, either; they lacked the vigor which seemed necessary for her pleasure.

Further adroit questioning along these lines brought out the information that Sally's sex life had been a busy one. It began at the age of nine, when her father attempted to rape her while he was drunk. Her mother had appeared on the scene in time to prevent actual rape from occurring, so that Sally emerged from this encounter more frightened than hurt. The mother had blamed Sally for "leading her father on," which was very confusing because of the injustice of the accusation. Her mother's further insistence that Sally pray for "the salvation of her soul" and for "God's forgiveness" made her angry. Several times Sally tried to rebel against praying; this resulted in her mother's flying into a frenzy, calling Sally such names as "spawn of the devil," telling her that she would be damned for eternity. Sally's only defense was to pretend to be praying, spending that time of silence in imagining ingenious tortures for her mother and planning on what she would do when she was independent.

When she was twelve, her father died of alcoholism, leaving her mother the sole support of the family. The mother worked very hard, scrimping and saving in order to permit Sally to continue with her education, sacrificing to buy Sally clothes so that she would "look as good as the other girls." The mother did not sacrifice in silence, however; at every opportunity she told Sally how much she was doing for her and how ungrateful Sally was.

When she was fourteen, Saly had her first affair with a man, and she had continued to have intercourse with every man possible since then. It wasn't always satisfactory in the sense that she could achieve orgasm, but it was exciting. As she expressed it, "Those experiences are mine, and nobody can take them away from me. And besides I get a kick out of making these men do what I want them to do— they look so silly sometimes."

In addition to all this sexual intercourse, she also masturbated—a practice which had begun shortly after the episode of attempted rape. With this she could always accomplish orgasm. It wasn't quite so satisfactory as having a man— but then men didn't seem to be as satisfactory as they should be, either. But it was fun, nevertheless—especially when they were exhausted and she was still eager.

She was careful not to mix her sexual escapades with her work; she had a good job with an excellent salary, and she was careful to behave in no way that would jeopardize her position. After work she had her own circle of acquaintances, among whom she enjoyed the reputation of being quite a "party girl." She told the doctor proudly about her sexual abilities—how one night she "wore out" five different men and was still going strong.

She had never met the man who could satisfy her, she said; if she could only find him, things would be different.

Sally's case, as you can see, was a rather difficult one. The things which she told about herself contained so much fantasy that it was quite a job to separate the wheat from the chaff. It took the doctor a long time to help her recognize the difference between fact and fancy.

Sally was a very frightened girl. No matter what actions she took, even during talking, she held her breath and went through it with as little contact as possible. It was apparent that she behaved in the same way during sex. Instead of reacting to the sensations which were present, she thought about other men and other times. Instead of feeling the actuality of the present, she reacted to her memories of the past and her fantasies of the future.

It soon became apparent to the doctor that Sally's sexual activity was a means of "getting even" with men, rather than a pleasure-giving, pleasure-receiving interchange. She apparently hated men and wanted to make them feel inferior—and yet she needed them desperately. It took longer for Sally to realize that she wasn't permitting her partners to satisfy her needs, but was sacrificing her own capacities for pleasure in order to obtain revenge. When she finally recognized this, she commented, "I'm doing just what Mama did with me—sacrificing myself and giving others hell because of it."

The turning point in her case was reached when she brought in a short story that she had written a few years previously. The central character was a kind, gentle man who solved the problems of a bewildered little girl. It was a beautiful piece of writing, with a tender sentiment which was quite in contrast to Sally's usual manner. When the doctor questioned her as to why she had chosen a kind man to be the hero, she broke down and sobbed for a long time. Finally she said, "I've always wanted to meet such a man, but I've never been able to find him. My father should have been that way—but he wasn't. He was cruel and selfish, just like all men. They're all alike—I hate them!"

With this emotional release she seemed to be able to become aware of her hatred and fear of all men, and to recognize that she was acting as if every man were going to try to rape her as her father had done, after which she would be punished as her mother had punished her. She interpreted her sexual behavior as a defense—if she "raped" the man first, then he couldn't rape her, and she wouldn't be punished.

This discussion covers only the high-points of Sally's case, of course. We omit the numerous side-line explorations of past situations, and do not mention all the ways in which Sally's sensory and emotional abilities were retrained. At the present time—almost two years after her first session—she is able to meet men without the compulsion to destroy them by exhausting them sexually. She has had numerous dates where she has been able to choose *not* to have intercourse, a choice which formerly she had never been able to make. Her personal appearance has improved markedly and her general health is much better. Her suicidal tendencies are a thing of the past, and she is planning for the future—her future—with interest and eagerness. True, she hasn't yet met the kind man of her youthful dreams—but she is learning that there is a reality of today which is as valid as any dream of childhood.

The homosexual person is one who has the body of one sex, but, during sexual activity, acts as if he were a member of the opposite sex. A male homosexual looks like a man, usually dresses like a man, acts like a man in ordinary, everyday conduct; but when he falls in "love," or when he wants to perform the love-act, he does not look for a member of the opposite sex—he chooses another man.

Homosexuality is not limited to men, of course—women can also be homosexual and can fall in "love" and make "love" with other women. We shall present a case history of each type later on, but first we want to discuss some of the generalities which apply to both the male and the female homosexual.

There is one observation of major importance: regardless of the extreme behavior of the homosexual and the definite pattern of sex expression which the homosexual practices, basically the problem is one of *fear*. If we search deeply enough, we can find the fear which is responsible for this deviation from "normal" behavior.

It may seem strange to say that a person is afraid and yet follows a pattern of action which holds more danger than what he is afraid of—and yet that is what seems to happen.

And yet is this so strange, after all? We have seen a person ashamed of something he has done who would rather have a beating than face what he most fears: his shame. We have seen children who seem to prefer being punished, who will even run away from home, rather than tell their parents of some minor misdeed which they have blown up to major proportions. Many homes have been broken up because the man or the woman has committed some minor infidelity; these people choose a broken home, rather than to admit the "shame" of what they have done.

Shame and fear are virtually synonymous. Neither of them can be measured objectively; their only significance lies in how the person feels. It may seem silly to you that your wife is afraid of lightning—but you may be afraid of a mouse.

Fear and shame depend upon a person's past experiences —and psychotherapy has found a way to deal with them. It has also found a way to help us find more rational, productive and meaningful ways to live; it does this by the reexamination of our subjective fears in the light of the present situation instead of the dark associations of the past.

The studies of psychotherapy suggest that our society unconsciously sets the stage for homosexual relations, meanwhile condemning the practice vigorously. With such confusion, is it surprising that sex deviations should flourish?

Observe the following: little boys are separated from little girls at an early age; any natural curiosity that arises is squelched or punished in some unreasonable fashion. As children grow older, the segregation persists, and now natural curiosity is evaluated as "criminal." In adult life this separation is insisted upon, unless marriage has taken place.

On the other hand, men are permitted to register at

hotels with men; the same goes for women—and no questions are asked. It would almost seem that society approves of what are called unnatural relations between man and man, and woman and woman.

To take it a step further, it would seem that society is so afraid of sex that the homosexual has been made the scapegoat in the general war against sex.

It is not the purpose of this book to begin a crusade against the unrealistic attitude of society toward the homosexual. It is necessary, however, that we review these attitudes in order to understand what sends multitudes of our citizens in the direction of "abnormal" sex behavior.

We do not regard the homosexual as a "pervert" or a "degenerate"—instead we think of him as a sick person, the product of his experiences, one who can change his way of doing things. It is hoped that by viewing him in this way we can help him to become a real person, an acceptable member who contributes to the progress of our society. Perhaps we can also help to change the attitudes which create an enemy who is capable of wrecking the human race.

It is valuable to know that homosexuality will respond to psychotherapy, that the pattern can be altered. It is even more valuable to know how it can be prevented. If you, as a parent, know that some of your attitudes toward your children are apt to produce homosexuality, you can change them. If you recognize that a child needs more than a good home, sufficient clothing and a balanced diet, you can supply these needs.

86

Let's consider the case of a homosexual man, in order to point out some of the deeds of omission and commission which were factors in his condition.

Larry was thirty-three years old; he was tall, blond and quite handsome in an effeminate way. His voice tones, his gestures, his mannerisms all emphasized that he was not like the usual male. Indeed, he made no attempt to deny his homosexuality, but admitted it frankly—even somewhat proudly.

When asked why he wanted psychotherapy, he spoke vaguely of a peculiar sense of unreality about the life he was leading. There was no real satisfaction in anything he did; his friends, who were also "queer," did not seem like people, but rather like "dressed-up marionettes."

This increasing sense of unreality about living was rather frightening, and his fears were also manifested in his dreams. He had nightmares about being pushed off a mountain top onto jagged rocks below, and he awoke from these dreams in a cold sweat of fear.

When the doctor asked him how he felt about all this, his answer was vague, and it was noticeable that he talked all around the subject. He had always enjoyed his homosexuality, he said, and he really didn't have any worries, financial or otherwise. It didn't disturb him because people made fun of him for being a "fairy," because he "knew" that all great artists and poets were "queer." Once in a while he had been beaten up by someone whom he had approached, but that didn't bother him, either—it was all part of the game.

"I guess that the only things which are really disturbing me are these damned nightmares and the rotten breaks I'm getting about making new friends. If you can get rid of those two things for me, I'll be happy," said Larry.

The doctor recognized this as an avoidance mechanism; he knew that therapy, to be successful, must deal with the entire personality structure, not with just one particular complaint. With such limitations on the goal of therapy, it would be a tremendously difficult task, so the doctor suggested that Larry consult someone else; he didn't want to take on his case under those circumstances.

At this point Larry became very disturbed; he broke into tears and pleaded with the doctor not to send him away.

"I've gone to other doctors," he sobbed, "and they all give me the brush-off. I guess I just have to face it—I've got to tell you the truth, even the truth that I've tried to hide from myself. I don't want to be a fairy—I'm a man, and I want to be a man. I like women—but every woman I've ever wanted has rejected me. I've got to find out why they always reject me."

With this change in Larry's attitude his treatment began. Several sessions were spent in considering and recalling the various experiences which might have led Larry to his present pattern of conduct. He recalled, with considerable agitation, a time when he was six years old; he and a little girl had been playing together and were innocently investigating each other's genitals, when the girl's mother caught them in the act. She became furious, called Larry all the nasty names she could think of, then whipped him severely.

After this she dragged him home to his mother and demanded that Larry be given another whipping.

Larry's mother, too, was horrified; she, too, whipped Larry and made him promise never to play with girls again. With this he was sent upstairs to bed, where he cried himself to sleep. Larry's father came home in the middle of the night, and was told of his son's "crime," whereupon he dragged Larry out of bed, gave him another beating and told him, "If I ever catch you playing with girls again, I'll kill you."

Larry was a very sick boy for a long time after this experience and some other equally distressing ones; he did a lot of thinking about them, of course, and came to a rather logical conclusion. As Larry, the man, expressed it to the doctor, "I guess I realized that if I didn't want to be hurt, I couldn't be myself—I just had to be somebody else. So I became the good little boy that my parents wanted me to be—but God, how I hated it!"

Yet there were advantages to having another self to present to the world—if any wrong was done, it was this other Larry who did it, and it was this other Larry who was punished. The "real" Larry was never punished, hence never felt any pain.

Incidentally, this peculiar splitting of a child's personality into the "good boy" and the "bad boy" is quite common: it seems to be the only way some children have of rationalizing the poorly-understood standards of "right" and "wrong" which their parents and the social order impose on them.

Larry recalled another incident which occurred when he was in high-school at the age of fourteen. There was a girl in his class who seemed to like him, who wasn't intolerant of his "sissified" behavior. Larry told about how he was fascinated with the swelling curves of her adolescent breasts, and how he used to day-dream about touching them. One day during school hours he found her standing in one of the alcoves off the hall, a place where there was little possibility of their being seen. He could no longer control his urge to put his arms around her, kiss her and attempt to fondle her breasts.

Apparently Larry had misjudged this girl's feelings toward him, for she screamed in terror. Teachers and pupils came running up to see what the trouble was, and there was a big furor raised about Larry's "criminal behavior." He was expelled from school, he was punished by his parents, and it was only after he had been made to promise faithfully that he'd never do anything like this again that he was admitted to a school in a different part of the city.

At this point Larry sighed and said, "I guess that this finally convinced me that women would always reject me."

"Tell me," asked the doctor, "have you ever been rejected by men? Have there ever been any times when you approached a man and were turned down?"

"Oh, yes—lots of times," was the answer, and Larry told of the many times when he had been beaten up, robbed, blackmailed and threatened with prosecution by different men with whom he had wanted to have sexual relations.

There were numerous—almost countless—examples of this sort of occurrence.

The doctor pointed out that "rejection" could hardly be a valid reason for avoiding woman and choosing men; the rejections by men had been much more numerous and much more painful.

"But these men didn't hurt *me*—they were hurting. . . ."

Larry's voice trailed off, as if he had suddenly become aware of the unreality of this "other-self" which he had created during his childhood. No matter what sort of a split he had in his personality it was undesirable that there were sensations associated with joys and sorrows, pleasures and pains.

This sudden recognition of false-to-fact associations, this burst of insight into one's own behavior patterns, is frequently encountered in psychotherapy. It takes more than insight, however, for lasting therapeutic effects to be gained. It is at this point that therapy can begin; the person can then re-train himself to react in ways other than his old habits. He can then learn to be aware of his sensations in order to make the most practical choice.

This is what happened in Larry's case. He no longer behaves as if women always and inevitably rejected him. He has had sexual experience with women and is now engaged to be married; his fiancee knows about his homosexuality, but is sufficiently intelligent to recognize it as a sort of prolonged adolescence out of which Larry is now maturing. He has had an occasional homosexual relation with one of his old friends, but there is no evidence of his returning to the constant search for new male lovers. In other words, Larry has become a man in his own right, secure in his feelings for the woman he loves.

Larry's case illustrates another point for discussion: the contrast between learning by trial, error and correction and being taught by social pressure. The infant, as he learns to walk and talk, does so by trying, by making mistakes and correcting them. For him there is no question of "right" and "wrong"—he just discovers that some ways are more effective than others.

Being taught customs and morals is much more complicated. The child is told that he "must" do the "right" things, "shouldn't" do the "wrong" things. "Right" and "wrong" and all their synonyms often seem illogical and arbitrary. It's confusing to the child—and we know that confusion leads to fear.

It seems pretty obvious that most members of our society, whether children or adult, are confused and fearful about sex.

We should like to illustrate this point further by discussing a case of a female homosexual. In the woman who falls in love only with other women, there is as much confusion as there is in the male counterpart. The same pattern of separation from self seems to exist; there is the creation of a substitute personality to absorb the punishment and to rebel in "freedom" against the injustices of the past.

Again we say that our concern is not based on moral evaluations. We observe, however, that the homosexual is involved in a struggle with morality—not the morality of society, but the morality of self. The female homosexual has a body which is rightly capable of certain functions, certain patterns of behavior—but she acts as if it were "wrong" to have them. She disowns her femaleness in order to become a "phony" male.

Assuming a masculine pattern of behavior will not make the female homosexual a man; she cannot escape the fact that she is a woman. If she could, she might attain a degree of peace in the pursuit of homosexuality—but observations show that this is not the case. Those who have observed numerous cases of women who would be men know that they are frustrated, miserable and unhappy.

We can even go a step further than this and say that they are so miserable and so confused that it is well-nigh impossible to predict their actions. Their confusion is so great that they are capable of destroying themselves and they might also destroy others, in creating their own self-destruction.

The destructive tendencies seem to stem from the frustration, the conflict which results from trying to achieve an impossible goal.

One goal of the female homosexual, like that of her "normal" sister, is the attainment of sex happiness—but she cannot reach it. This is *not* because of the opinions of society, nor is it because of unfortunate selection of her sex partner, nor any other of the specious "reasons" so often given; it is because of her femininity, which reaches out for male love.

In most discussions of homosexuality, the emphasis is placed on the oddity of the behavior pattern. We shall try to stress the experiences which might account for such behavior, and to show how the behavior-pattern fails to fulfill the needs of the person.

In order to do so, we would like to tell you about Martha. She consulted a psychotherapist because she was plagued with migraine. Everything was all right except those headaches. Oh, she had nights when she couldn't get to sleep, but that didn't matter because she had her sleeping pills to fall back on. She probably drank more than she should, too, but that was unimportant because, as she said, "Drinking is fun; it helps me to forget just about everything."

She went into great detail about these headaches and told how they were related to her menstrual periods, to emotional stresses, to "nervousness"; in discussing this she also mentioned casually that she was homosexual and had been ever since adolescence.

"Do you suppose," the doctor asked, "that these headaches might be related to your homosexuality?"

"Absolutely not," was Martha's indignant reply. "You doctors are all alike. Why do you have to assume that lesbianism is unnatural? Why should it be less natural for two women to love each other than for a man and a woman to love each other? How stupid can you doctors get?"

The doctor's eyebrows raised slightly at this, but he made no comment.

94

"Why do you doctors think that you know it all? I know what I want—I want to get rid of my headaches, and I don't want to be bothered by talking about irrelevancies."

It was obvious that Martha's response was far more agitated than was warranted by the simple questions which had been asked. Her general appearance, the tone of her voice, the arbitrariness of her demands, indicated that she was acting more like a child having a temper-tantrum than like a mature woman.

The doctor recognized this and merely sat quietly. Like the child whose temper tantrum has been ignored, Martha finally came around to the point of asking forgiveness. It was as if she knew that the doctor wouldn't give in to her indignation or to her "superior" knowledge.

"I suppose that I'm wrong," she sighed. "God knows I've tried to work this out for myself—and I haven't been able to do it. I'm sorry, Doctor—I shouldn't have blown my top like that. All right—I'm willing to try it your way."

With Martha's assent, the process of investigation of her life began. She had been brought up in a small midwestern city, where both of her parents taught in the public schools. They were unemotional people, she said, who emphasized the value of "clear thinking" and "proper behavior." These ideals didn't prevent them from criticizing their neighbors, however, and Martha recalled how much she used to be annoyed by her parents' malicious gossiping.

She didn't feel that her parents had wanted her; she frequently heard them tell their friends that "Martha was an accident." Nor did it add to her feelings of being wanted to be told, "It's too bad that you weren't a boy." Her father said, and her mother agreed, that it was a man's world and that most women—especially the motherly, house-wifely type—were stupid, no better than cows.

There was no affection shown around Martha's home; both her parents seemed to abhor any demonstrations of love. The only time her parents paid much attention to her was when she was punished, which was all too frequently. Martha also remembered that at the end of every whipping her mother would say, "There—that'll teach you not to be a foolish girl."

Martha wasn't permitted to bring any playmates home; whenever she tried to develop a friendship with another child, she would be told, "You don't want to play with that sort of riff-raff." She tried to rebel against this devaluation of her friends, but her objections were always over-ridden. Her personality gradually changed; at first she used to envy the kids who had so much fun playing together, but later her envy turned to bitter hatred and criticism.

Martha was, needless to say, a solitary child; she had very few pleasures in life until, with the onset of adolescence, she discovered the sensations which accompany masturbation.

She used to masturbate frequently; it became part of her going-to-sleep program, and she also used it as a means of consolation whenever she had a disagreement with her parents. It wasn't until years later that she found out that her activities were called "masturbation," so she didn't relate them to wrong-doing particularly; all she knew about -

it at that time was that it was pleasurable and a secret to be kept to herself. She was certain that her mother would disapprove if she found out about it, so she was careful not to be caught.

About a year after this a new girl moved into the neighborhood. Betty was almost the exact opposite of Martha; she was friendly, jovial and affectionate. During Betty's first few days at school Martha had tried to take her around and help her get acquainted; she enjoyed doing this because she could feel superior to a stranger. Before many weeks had passed Betty had been accepted by the group to a much greater extent than Martha ever had—and this, of course, aroused Martha's envy again.

Betty was a staunch ally of Martha's; when the other boys and girls used to make fun of Martha's peculiar ways and different appearance, Betty would defend her loyally.

"I didn't quite know how to take this," Martha said. "I liked her because she was nice to me—but I used to hate her, too. She was everything I wanted to be. There were times when I used to spend all my allowance on her, and other times when I wouldn't speak to her for days. It never seemed to matter to her how I acted—she was always sweet to me."

It was part of Betty's disposition to be demonstrative and affectionate, and Martha didn't know quite how to react to the kisses and hugs which were bestowed on her. She was both attracted and repelled by the idea of contact with another girl, especially since it caused a turmoil in her own feelings.

97

One day when Martha's parents were safely out of the house, she invited Betty in; a casual kiss prompted Martha to start a further exploration, the same sort of exploring that she did on her own body under the bed-clothes at night. Betty made no objection—instead her attitude seemed to be one of "Do with me as you will."

"It gave me the strangest feeling," said Martha. "I felt so strong—I felt like a man does. I just wanted to squeeze her until she cried. I wanted to eat her up. And I didn't have any sexual feelings, either—it didn't seem important for me to get any satisfaction out of it. It was so much better to have the feeling that I could play with Betty like she was a little puppy, that I could make her do whatever I wanted to—just as if she was a marionette and I had all the strings in my hands. It was wonderful to feel so powerful."

It was obvious that this experience had made a very vivid impression on Martha. She was able to go into minute details of description of how Betty had acted. She told how Betty's face would get warm and flushed, but that her lips would be cold; how Betty would breathe more and more rapidly until she sighed, moaned and shook her head from side to side with ecstasy of orgasm.

Martha dwelt on the details of this to such an extent that it was apparent that she was evading something. After the question, "What happened next?" had been asked several times by the doctor, the reason for the evasion became clear: Matha's mother had suddenly walked in while the girls were in the midst of their play. All hell broke loose:

she screamed at Betty, told her to get out and never come back again. She called Betty a pervert, a degenerate, and a few other names which are not usually heard in polite society.

Martha was astounded at this. She had never seen her mother act this way before; here was this woman, so proud of her "self-control" and "objectivity," who never showed any flicker of emotion, suddenly turned into a distraught, screaming female.

"It was a funny thing," Martha remarked, "But that made me feel strong, too. Mother whipped me as hard as she could—but it didn't bother me at all."

Martha told how her mother, exhausted by the efforts to beat her into some show of repentance, finally broke into tears and sobbing. It was a show of emotion that had always been condemned—tears were the sign of a weakling, no strong person ever cries. Martha felt she was stronger than her mother—even stronger than her father.

This experience seemed to set the pattern for Martha's homosexuality: her partners were girls she could dominate, who would respond to her caresses in the way she wanted them to respond. She seldom got any sexual pleasure herself from these relationships; she still obtained her satisfaction by masturbating. The feeling of mastery, of power, of "masculine strength," as she put it, seemed much more important than her own sexual sensations.

This story did not come out all at once, of course; it came out in bits and pieces which are put together coherently in this report. It took months of careful and serious questioning, especially since the original incidents had seemingly been forgotten.

It took time, also, for Martha to recognize her pattern of looking for "weak" girls, so she could dominate them and thereby gain the feelings of "power" and "strength" which were so important to her. As her therapy progressed she found it possible to cease looking for this false "strength" and to find a real strength in herself as a woman.

She recalled how often she used to pray for the strength to be weak like the women with whom she found sex pleasure, and how she was always afraid to show her weakness.

It took a longer time for her to recognize that she wanted to be loved by man—but that came, too.

She felt that she was able to explain her headaches on this basis, too—her migraine attacks were a form of "weakness," the only weakness which she could permit herself to show. Perhaps her explanation was not entirely correct—but it was *her* explanation. With this "reason," and with her re-awakening femininity, her headaches ceased to trouble her.

This probing into the past was not the only form of therapy which she received. We have discussed only this phase of it in order to bring out a certain point—*there are reasons for becoming a homosexual.*

These reasons seem to fall into a rather definite pattern: an experience (or experiences) in which the person learned that it was better, or safer, or more productive of feelings of strength, to have sexual relations with persons of the same gender. With this goes a repression of the normal outlets for love and affection which are inherent in every one of us; when love doesn't come out with the opposite sex, it will turn into homosexual channels or other deviations.

We might also mention here that these cases may sound melodramatic. They are—and it is just this sort of melodrama which seems to be a part and parcel of homosexuality. These individuals are dramatists; their entire lives seem to be theatrical performances. The recognition that life is not necessarily a stage, and that they don't have to be actors seems to be important in therapy; when they learn their own sensations and can thereby establish their own reality, their homosexuality ceases to be a problem.

HOW TO MAKE THE MOST OF SEX

The heading of this section is, admittedly, rather misleading. It sounds as if we are going to teach you how to do something—how to be more potent, how to get more enjoyment out of sexual relations, or how to increase your capacities for sexual expression.

But this, as we see it, would be impossible; if it were possible, it would certainly be impractical in a book of this type.

It is impossible because knowledge of sex is acquired through personal sensory experience—a person learns about sex by teaching himself, rather than by having someone

101

else tell him what to do, or by being told that he *should* do thus-and-so.

We shall therefore limit our discussion to two phases: first, the attitudes and beliefs which tend to block sexual expression and enjoyment and secondly, how these blocks may be overcome. Perhaps some of the things we say will be in disagreement with your ideas; if that is the case you don't have to accept them. In any event, it won't hurt to give this subject some consideration; it might be that a re-examination of some of your basic beliefs will enable you to change them, if you want to change.

Let us begin by pointing out once again that Man is a sexual being: sex is necessary for his survival. It makes no difference how we choose to evaluate sex, as "good" or "evil"; we are, nevertheless, born with the organs and the potential function of reproduction.

But sex is *not* just the act of reproduction—it is an emotion of pleasure, it is a sensory relationship between two people, it is a basic, inherent need which is going to find an outlet, no matter how we try to curb it. Sex is a relationship which can be experienced and enjoyed, which can give us a strength of living, a satisfaction in living.

When we look around us, however, we see that the potentialities of sex are realized only too seldom. Instead we see guilt, shame and repugnance; we see sex regarded as an unpleasant duty, or as a joyless necessity, or as a bestial activity to be avoided as much as possible.

In studying sexual aberrations we are sure to find conflict and confusion: conflict between what a person feels and what he is told he *should* feel, confusion between his own feelings and what he thinks his feelings ought to be.

We believe that the concept of sex as "evil" is one of the more important obstacle to the enjoyment of life. The concept is so deeply imbedded in our ways of speaking that we often overlook it—but it's there. For example, we refer to anecdotes about sex as "dirty" stories or "smutty" jokes. We set up censorship to make certain that young minds shall not be "polluted" by references to sex.

Why should this most vital and pleasurable of functions be considered unclean? Isn't there some other attitude which can be taken? Is it necessarily true that knowledge about sex will make a person a sex maniac? Isn't there some other choice than licentiousness or repression?

From the doctor's viewpoint, sex is not evil. It is a reaching out of life for life in order to perpetuate life. It is beyond evil—and when we recognize this, we can all find greater health, joy and freedom.

Consider what happens when sex is identified as evil. A large proportion of our society says that sex is "dirty"— and what happens? We see guilt—shame—unnatural conduct—feelings of inferiority—loss of contact with reality. Is it just a coincidence that there is frequently a loss of sex function in schizophrenia? Is it a coincidence that many murderers are sexually repressed?

We believe that when the sex instinct is permitted to develop freely and naturally, a man becomes a happier, more moderate, more loving person. We don't believe that

Man is evil or promiscuous; given a chance, he will be moderate, outgoing and friendly. We believe that it is the restrictions which are placed on us that lead to uncontrollable evil.

As a matter of fact, Man takes better care of his animals than he does of himself. He knows that animals which are deprived of natural sexual outlets will either become sick or unmanageable. What, then, can Man expect of himself when he restricts his own natural functions?

What do you suppose happens when a child is taught that sex is "wicked" and "dirty"? In one case, a patient with an unusually good memory of his childhood told how there was a period of confusion and unhappiness which lasted for months when he found out where babies come from. He had been told that anybody who had anything to do with sex was wicked—and when he discovered that his own existence was the result of his parents' "wickedness," he just couldn't reconcile the two ideas. He loved his parents, deeply and sincerely—but they were "bad" by reason of what they had done, and this lesson of evil they themselves had taught him!

This dilemma, carried into adulthood, gave him a confused idea of women. They were either sexless angels or prostitutes. He was able to resolve this confusion when he became aware of his own sexual feelings and develop his own evaluations of sex.

If a child has been taught that sex is evil, this "knowledge" is hard to ignore when he grows up and is married. He tries to find sex-expression with his wife—but feelings

of guilt plague him. He has been taught that sex is "wicked"
—how can he partake of it with love?

The experience of every psychotherapist demonstrates
more and more the relationship between early sexual education and adult behavior. There was the man who was
arrested time after time for beating his wife; he did it, he
said, because she acted like a whore. When asked for an
explanation of this, he said that she enjoyed the sex act
and he didn't think that was right; no decent woman would
have such feelings. After each beating he would be ashamed
and repentant, and would promise his wife and the court
never to repeat this conduct—but he was apparently unable
to keep his promises.

During psychotherapy it came out that his parents had
drummed into him with beatings and sermons that sex was
evil. He also said that his only premarital sexual experience
was in houses of prostitution. With such knowledge, it was
logical for him to treat his wife in this fashion, so logical
that it took a long time and a lot of hard work both for him
and his therapist before he could act as if that weren't the
only attitude he could have toward sex.

Another concept which is common and hampering to
sex happiness is the fear of the stranger. Children are
warned to be wary of strangers, to fear them and avoid
them. They are taught that they can be safe only within
their own family circle, that "outsiders" aren't interested in
them, that they shouldn't bother with people whom they
don't know.

With such training, a child soon gets an exaggerated

and somewhat unrealistic idea of relationships with people other than those in a small circle. He is told he can't trust people outside his family—whom then can he trust?

Perhaps this is a reason for the tendency of many women to marry men who resemble their fathers, for men to marry the women who are most like their mothers. It seems obvious that such a choice is not necessarily the best one from the standpoint of growth and happiness.

Our experiences, especially those in the field of international relationships, seem to demonstrate that *xenophobia*, the fear of the stranger, is a great stumbling-block to mutual understanding and harmony. Why, then, should we foster this fear to such an extent? It has been said that there aren't any strangers—there are only people whom we haven't tried to know.

Perhaps if we would mingle a little more, and exchange our thoughts and feelings a little more freely, we might have a greater opportunity for happiness. We might also be in a better position to find the sort of mate with whom we could be happy, instead of repeating a family pattern of frustration.

Another concept which acts as a barrier to sex happiness is the opinion that feelings are wrong, that emotions are a function which should be repressed. Emotions—evaluations —are as much a part of our orientation in this world as the sense perceptions which keep us from bumping into furniture or the visual discrimination between red and green. They are, indeed, the very determinants of happiness or unhappiness. Yet we are taught repeatedly to deny or "control" them, and beyond that, to ignore the sense perceptions on which they rest.

Compare this with the usual sort of training given to children in many American homes and schools: Don't show your feelings! Don't be so demonstrative! Don't be so emotional!

But we are emotional; we having feelings; we like to be demonstrative. We're humans, and we come into this world equipped with emotions and feelings. We can repress them, refuse to let them function one way—but we can't eliminate them. If we try to act as if we didn't have emotions, we become confused. The case histories have shown how people act when they have this confusion.

The greatest confusion seems to result when we feel one way and are told that we *should* feel in an entirely different way. Take the case of Sally who had been brought up with lots of information about how she ought to feel. When she finally cut her ties with home and began her search for "freedom," the confusion still persisted. She rebelled against the sexual taboos by being promiscuous, yet the confusion about what she "should" feel prevented her from knowing what she *did* feel.

She considered herself as an "emancipated" woman—but the only freedom she had was a freedom away from the enjoyment of living. She could prove her independence by having sexual relations with every man who came along, but she couldn't get pleasure or satisfaction out of these affairs.

Enough of this. There is another point we want to make before winding up this discussion.

So far we have pointed out repeatedly that the child who isn't permitted to express his feelings is a candidate for adult neurosis. We have shown how a certain type of sex education in childhood seems to result in a typical pattern of sexual behavior in adulthood. We have mentioned that early negative evaluations of sex are followed later by confusion about sex.

We have, in other words, suggested that parents are largely responsible for the behavior of their children. But this doesn't mean that we're trying to make parents feel guilty, or that they should be ashamed of the "terrible mistakes" which they made.

After all, the parents of today are the children of yesterday, and their confusions were a result of the confusions of the previous generation. If we were going to blame anyone, we would have to go back generation by generation and lay all the blame on our primordial ancestors. But what good would that do?

There is something which can be done—something which can help us, as parents, to keep from imposing on our children the confusions of our own parents. It's not too difficult, either; we can start the process of improvement with this question: do I want my child to have the same sort of sex education I had? What was I told about sex? What kind of information did I get—realistic or unrealistic? Was sex a horrible secret or was it a natural process?

It's not just a question of teaching—it's also a question of showing. We refer to the showing of affection, the affection that every parent feels for a child.

It appears as if many parents hesitated to show affection to a child because they have confused affection with sexual desire. Let's not be afraid of a word—there is probably a sexual aspect in every demonstration of love, but every demonstration of love does not lead to sexual intercourse. The quality of sex that is in a mother's love for her child is completely different from the quality of sex that is in the love she feels for her husband. In order for a child to grow to be an adult, capable of love, the inspiration which comes from the warmth and vitality of the sex quality in the parents' love must be known. Parents need not worry that this might lead to incest; it cannot.

It's never too late for another evaluation of your past teachings and your present beliefs. Perhaps your childhood sex education was good; could you improve it for your children? Perhaps your sex education was not so good; can't you learn from your parents' mistakes?

Supposing, instead of saying that parents are responsible for the sexual aberrations of their children, we say that society is to blame. Suppose that we say, "Yes, that's the way things are—we can't change them. I can change, of course—but nobody else will, so why should I?"

It is the opinion of this author that society can be changed. It would be even more correct to say that society *does* change; it changes and grows, just as the individuals who comprise it change and grow. Society is made up of people; as the people modify their ways of living, so does society modify its views.

You, as an individual, can change your ideas about sex. If enough of you want to change, then society will change. The problem can best be solved by having each one of us try to solve his own problem, and by each of us helping the others to solve their problems.

We believe that the key to the problem can be found in our feelings, our needs and our expressions. It has been observed countless times that a patient who has a "sex block" can overcome it to a considerable degree when he becomes aware of his feelings and sensations. When he gets to the point where he can say, "This is I; I am feeling this; what do I want to do about it?" he is well on the road to recovery.

We have also observed that when this awareness of feeling begins in one area, it extends itself to all other areas of emotion. The person doesn't only lose his troubles; he is enriched by the wealth of his feelings, liberated by the enjoyment of his own senses.

Nor is he alone in this richer, freer life. With it goes an understanding of the wonderful sensation of togetherness. This is what happens when we aren't afraid of others.

When we learn how to take down our barriers of fear, we can experience the joys of contact; we can feel excited, we can laugh, we can live and enjoy living.

CHAPTER VI

THE INSIDE STORY OF ALLERGIES, ULCERS AND GLANDS

RESPIRATORY (ASTHMA, HAY FEVER, SINUSITUS, ETC.) · GAS-TRO-INTESTINAL (STOMACH ULCERS, COLITIS, ETC.) · MUSCULO-SKELETAL (ARTHRITIS, RHEUMATISM, ETC.) · GLANDULAR (SKIN DISEASES, OBESITY, UNDER-DEVELOPMENT, ETC.)

WE now come to the point where we can begin to talk a little more specifically about psychosomatic illnesses. The groundwork has been laid, and by now you are more familiar with the various aspects of the sort of diseases which is "all in the mind."

In order to talk about these diseases in a more systematic fashion, we shall consider the various groups of functions:

111

we shall talk about respiratory disturbances, gastro-intestinal disturbances, disturbance of the various systems such as the musculo-skeletal, the glandular and so on. It's convenient to speak about the various parts of the human being this way, and it has become even more convenient because this is the way in which we have learned about the human being in school.

We must not lose sight of the fact, however, that the human being *works as a whole*. We cannot have a person with a disordered stomach and nothing else; rather, we have a disordered person whose complaints are chiefly directed toward the stomach—but with many other disorders of function besides. The medical profession has recognized this in their descriptions of the typical ulcer personality, even in observing that patients with stomach ulcers are apt to have a characteristic similarity of body build and general appearance.

So when we speak about a psychosomatic disease of a certain organ or a disorder of function of a certain system, you can remember that we are talking about only one aspect of a complex set of interrelationships. To make a comparison, when we look at a cube, we don't see all six faces simultaneously—but we can look at one or two faces without forgetting that there are more than just these. We can talk about one face of the cube at one time—it's easier to do it that way—but if we are to understand the cube-as-a-whole completely, we shall remember the other five faces, plus the edges, plus the angles, plus some speculation as to what is at the center of the cube.

RESPIRATORY DISEASES

The first system we shall consider as a site of psycho-somatic disease will be the respiratory system. This includes the nostrils, the lining of the nasal cavity, the turbinates (which are bony protrusions from the sides of the nasal cavity; they act to increase the surface of mucous membrane exposed to the incoming air), the paranasal sinuses, the pharynx, the larynx, the trachea, the larger bronchi and the smaller bronchioles and the alveoli, which are the little air-sacs in which the function of the lungs takes place. We might also consider the vocal cords as part of the respiratory system, as it requires the passage of air to set them into vibration. The muscles which attach to the ribs and that dome-shaped muscle called the diaphragm also take part in respiration. Even at this simple level of description we can see how one system overlaps and is intermingled with another—that they can be separated in *speaking* about them, but they cannot be separated in actuality.

Now, what are the functional disorders of the respiratory tract? The common cold, chronic sinus trouble, hay fever, and asthma are the common conditions. Inasmuch as this book deals with principles rather than with the treatment of any specific condition, we shall omit any discussion of the more rare conditions, meanwhile remembering that they can be psychosomatic in origin also.

Mac was a patient with asthma. He had had this condition for over thirty years, his first attack having occurred while he was an infant. Like a typical asthmatic, his breathing difficulties became more severe during hay-fever season, beginning in mid-August, and whenever he had a cold. He had had the usual medical treatments—drugs to relax the spasm of his bronchial passages, drugs to liquefy the thick, tenacious mucus; he had even taken such hormones as cortisone and ACTH (the adrenocorticotrophic hormone of the anterior pituitary). In spite of all these measures—and note that all of these treatments came from *outside* the patient—he was seldom more than fairly comfortable. He was able to work only about half the time, and as a result was never able to keep the sort of job which his superior abilities permitted.

There were numerous ways in which he could have been treated; there was the medical angle, of course, but that had been tried and found to be unsuccessful over a period of years. It was therefore decided to approach his condition more from the psychological viewpoint.

In the treatment of a psychological condition there are two aspects of the person to consider: one, he has had numerous experiences from which he has learned to be the way he is; two, the way he is.

It is a peculiar and paradoxical state of affairs, but very few people know how they are acting; when they become aware of what they are doing, they become able to act in some other way. Let's look at that idea again—it is simple and fundamental, and yet it is a difficult one for most people to grasp.

Mac had asthma; he breathed in a certain set pattern. He acted as if that were the *only* way in which he could breathe—and yet he was not aware that *he* was breathing in that way!

This idea can be stated in another way: in order for a person to be able to choose between doing or not doing a certain action, he must be able both to perform that action and not to perform that action. A man who has no legs cannot choose *not* to walk—he has no choice in the matter. A choice implies two or more alternatives; when there is no alternative, there is no possibility of choosing.

Now, in Mac's case, he was acting as if he had no choice except to breathe asthmatically. We all know that this is an incorrect way to act; if it were correct, everyone would have asthma. Moreover, there were times when Mac was free from asthma—so he did have a choice between acting asthmatically and not acting asthmatically at some times.

The first step in his treatment, then, was to teach him how to have asthma! When he was told that this would be done, he received the statement with scepticism; he was polite about it, but one could see that he regarded it as ridiculous. His scepticism diminished considerably, however, when he found out that he didn't know how he was breathing during an asthmatic attack! He was not aware that he pulled up his shoulders, nor that he had a fixed, unchanging respiratory rate, or that he had a little half-smile on his face, or that his skin itched during an attack, or that he felt both angry and pleased while he wheezed.

He spent several hours in learning how he breathed, how he felt, how he acted in general while in the throes of his respiratory difficulties. He learned how to produce the sounds of an asthmatic wheeze by tightening up the muscles around his larynx, and he came to recognize how the muscles in the back of his neck also became tense as he did so. He learned that he did not pause between the end of inhalation and the beginning of exhalation; instead he changed from air-intake to air-output as rapidly as a ball is bounced off the sidewalk. He learned, in short, that he could produce an attack of asthma any time he wanted it— and was thereby enabled to a considerable degree to choose between having asthma and not having asthma!

It was also necessary to consider how he got asthma in the first place. In a previous discussion we showed that people learn by experience; the assumption was therefore made that there was a time in Mac's life when he breathed asthmatically, when he couldn't breathe in any other way, when it seemed that he was able to keep on living because he was able to breathe that way. So a search was made for the experience or experiences which taught him that asthmatic breathing is a life-saving action.

At this point it becomes necessary to digress in order to discuss a rather new viewpoint. Most people assume that that intellectual activity which we call memory starts at about the age of three. In the type of psychiatric approach with which Mac's case was treated, it was assumed that he could remember anything that happened at any time throughout his entire existence. Note carefully what was said—it was *assumed* that he could remember, not that he *could* remember. Research has shown that making this assumption leads to benefits; whether it is true or not seems to make little if any difference.

So Mac was asked, "When do you suppose you first had difficulty in breathing? When do you suppose that you *could have had* asthmatic-type respirations?"

"Gee, I don't know," Mac answered. "My mother told me that I had my first attack of asthma when I was about nine months old. My older brother and sister took me to where they were loading wheat, and they forgot about me and left me in a box car for about an hour. I guess it was pretty dusty in there—but I don't remember anything about it."

The next question was: "Assuming that you could remember what went on when you were nine months old, what do you suppose that you'd notice?"

Mac discussed the probabilities of this situation at great length with the therapist, and as he did so it was observed that with each association he brought up his asthma would first become more noticeable, then would become less intense. For example, he assumed that he cried while he sat in the dusty box-car; he imitated the cry of a baby and the asthmatic wheezing promptly became louder. A few more infantile wails and he began to chuckle at the incongruity of himself, a thirty-five-year-old man, crying like a baby—then the wheezing subsided.

His therapy continued, with both the "how" and the "why" of his illness being considered. He was helped to an awareness of *how* he acted to produce the complex activity called asthma. Then he was helped to discuss an experience wherein he might have learned that asthmatic activities were valuable. The value of having asthma was also considered—what did he get by having asthma that he wouldn't get if he didn't have this condition?

Some very odd answers come up when people are asked questions such as this, especially if the person brings out the first answer without considering how much sense it makes. Mac was asked, "What would happen if you didn't breathe asthmatically?" His answer was, "I wouldn't breathe—and then I'd die." Anyone who is capable of thinking can recognize that such a response is irrational and contrary to fact. If Mac didn't breathe asthmatically, he could also breathe slowly, or rapidly, or regularly, or irregularly, or in numerous other ways. But he viewed his asthmatic breathing as if it were the *only* way in which he could breathe.

Mac's progress towards recovery was slow but consistent. At first he was able only to respond verbally. He could say, "All right, so I don't have to have asthma." But he would still be breathing with forcible exhalations and would wheeze with each respiration. He could accept the therapist's statement on the verbal level but not on the actional level; he knew the words but he couldn't make the actions fit the words as yet.

Mac's case illustrates how psychosomaticists differ with

those who have a more conventional medical orientation. The average doctor acts as if he should do everything in his power to stop the course of illness, meanwhile emphasizing that there is an illness. The doctor who is more interested in the patient than in the disease is aware that *illness is a means of surviving*: instead of trying *only* to shorten the course of illness, he also tries to help the patient understand how and why he became ill, and to enable him to recognize that he has a choice between this method of survival and other methods.

And what happened to Mac? At the time of writing this he is still continuing to show improvement. He is becoming aware of the various emotional factors of his asthma—that it is a means of expressing anger, or grief, or fear, or disgust. He is learning how to express these emotions in more appropriate channels, learning how to cry, how to clench his fists and tense his jaw muscles, how to tremble. He went through a hay-fever season without having to be hospitalized as in previous years. His need for medications is becoming less and less. Absences from work have been less frequent and of shorter duration—and this occurred within about fifteen sessions given over a period of less than six months.

Judging from patients with similar conditions and with similar forms of treatment, he can expect to continue to improve, and, having done so, to keep his gains without recurrence of his illness.

It has been calculated that the common cold has been responsible for more lost man-hours of labor than any other illness or accident. Almost everybody gets a cold once in a while—or at least if he doesn't get one, he expects that he will.

Millions of dollars have been spent in research for the causes of colds and for remedies which will cure them. Various aphorisms are used to describe the attitude of therapeutic hopelessness, such as, "If you treat a cold properly, it will last for fourteen days; if you don't treat it, it will last for two weeks."

Very few people have considered that the common cold could be a self-created, psychosomatic illness—and therefore unnecessary! The immediate objection to this statement is to point out all the work which has been done on the cold as an infectious disease: the isolation of the filterable virus which can be transmitted from one person to another. And then there is the commonly cited observation of the people who live in isolated communities near the Arctic circle: all winter long, while they are snowed in, nobody has a cold, but when the first ship arrives in the spring, everyone gets a cold. There is also the firm belief that being around somebody who has a cold will lead to your "catching" cold—again implying that the sole source is the virus which is transmitted from the cold-sufferer to the unwilling recipient of the unwanted gift.

In addition to this is the list of beliefs as to the prevention of colds. To prevent a cold, stay out of drafts, don't let yourself become chilled, get plenty of sleep and so on.

Perhaps these are all important factors—but there may be some other ones as well. Have you ever considered that the sounds of a cold tend to put you in a receptive state for getting a cold? Have you ever made the observation in a theater that when one person starts coughing, he seems to start a chorus of coughs?

Let's consider the symptoms of a cold from the stand-point of the sounds which go along with it, and see what other states there are in which these sounds are produced. First there are the sniffles—the sudden inhalation through the nose in an attempt to draw the mucus back into the nasal passages. We also hear sniffling when a person is crying. Then there's the explosive clearing of the throat; if we watch the persons who clear their throats often, we notice that the action is usually accompanied by a frown or a scowl—and doesn't that throat-clearing noise sound something like a growl? And the cough—that sound is frequently compared with the sound of a dog barking, which is the dog's method of saying, "I'm suspicious of you."

In other words, some of the sounds of a cold might be interpreted as non-verbal expressions of emotion, especially the emotions of grief, rage and fear. That reminds us of other observations, such as the fact that a large portion of the mourners at a funeral will come down with colds a few days later, or that a child who becomes angry or otherwise disturbed is apt to get a case of the sniffles. Indeed, it has long been known that any highly emotional experience is often followed by a so-called "upper respiratory infection"; have you ever notice the frequency of colds among the people who have recently been married?

And what is this supposed to prove? Well, it's not intended to *prove* anything—but this is a way to point out that there might be other factors at work in the production of the common cold than those which are usually suspected. And, if such is the case, we have another point of attack at this common, annoying condition. Put it this way: if a person coughs near you and gives you a few million bacteria, you can't do much about it, unless you want to go around with a portable air-filtration system. But if it is the *sound* of a cough which makes you want to imitate that sound, and if you can best imitate that sound by developing a congestion of the respiratory tract, then you have a choice. You don't have to imitate that sound if you don't want to.

This raises the question of why a person should want to imitate a cough. The idea of "wanting" to be ill is frequently mentioned by psychiatrists in their attempts to explain the presence of disease, and is almost as often rejected by the patients.

It would be more accurate to say that some people act *as if* they wanted a certain symptom or a complex of symptoms. In general, "wanting" something is the first step towards getting it; therefore, if you got a cold, you wanted it.

The theme of this book would express this concept in a slightly different way. There was a time when your lungs felt congested and your bronchial tubes were filled with mucus; you coughed, and heard the sound of the cough. Sound of cough, act of coughing and the sensations which are a stimulus to coughing were all experienced simultaneously and were, in this situation, equivalent. And so, when you hear someone else coughing, you may "want" to cough, too.

There are exceptions to this, of course; some people can listen to coughing all day without the slightest urge to empty their lungs explosively. In this case it might be said that they do not have the fixed association between sound of cough and act of cough that the chronic coughers do.

The various signs and symptoms of the common cold can be related to other activities as well. As is mentioned elsewhere, one way that we can look at psychosomatic illness is that it is a non-verbal communication or expression of a bodily state. If you want to tell someone that you are angry, you can express it in words, "I'm angry," or, "I'm annoyed." You can also frown, thrust your jaw forward, clench your fists and growl—and there are few who would mistake the meaning of your message.

And what message would you be imparting by having the symptoms of a cold? It might be that your sniffling and runny nose are a means of imitating crying, of saying non-verbally, "I am sad." The watery eyes would make this message more obvious. Or we might say that the cough, which empties the respiratory passages, the drainage from the nose, the weeping eyes all betoken an attempt at getting rid of some irritant—such as one's wife, or one's boss, or the necessity for appearing at some undesirable social function. Or a cold may mean many other messages besides these—you can figure them out, if you so desire.

When the doctor looks at a patient who has "sinus trouble," he sees practically the same picture as is seen during the common cold. Sinusitis is usually one phase of the cold, disappearing as the other cold symptoms subside. In this situation we speak of an acute inflammation of the sinuses.

When most people talk about sinus trouble, they are referring to the condition known as chronic sinusitis. In this there is a constant low-grade infection of the mucus membrane which lines the sinus-cavities in the bones of the face. The openings of the sinuses become swollen and the mucus cannot drain out; when this happens, the person has a headache. Or the sinuses may suddenly begin to drain; the mucus then drips down the back of the throat, causing a chronic, tickly cough. The swallowing of infected mucus may lead to nausea and vomiting; the presence of infection may lead to inflammation of the tonsils and adenoids.

This is the way sinus trouble looks to the general practitioner; how does it look to the psychosomaticist?

We would ask these questions about sinusitis: how does the person go about getting sinus trouble? What types of emotional stress affect the disease? What are the advantages of having sinus trouble? What emotions might he be expressing with his symptoms? What emotions is he repressing?

124

We have noticed that one factor may be a definite relationship between sinus infection and grief, between the amount of nasal congestion and the number of unshed tears in a person's life. It certainly seemed to be so in the case of Helen.

Helen was not a very attractive girl; when one looked at her, the first thing one saw was a large, red nose with irritated nostrils. The nose was frequently buried in a wad of tissue—but if you couldn't see it, you could hear it.

Helen's reason for psychotherapy was not her sinus trouble; that was just one of her numerous complaints. It was obvious, however, that all her complaints followed a definite pattern: she didn't seem to know how to let out. She was constipated; her menstrual periods were scanty; her skin was dry; she wheezed slightly as she exhaled; according to her, she never cried, she never got angry, and it was hard for her to laugh. All her avenues for letting things out of her body seemed to be shut up.

One day during her therapy she recalled a time when her mother had shut her up in a dark closet as punishment for being "naughty." Helen didn't think that she had been naughty, and felt that her mother was being extremely unjust. She was also frightened at being left alone in that dark, musty-smelling place; there was no telling what might be lurking under those shapeless masses of coats.

As she recounted this experience and tried to get the feeling of being shut up, she suddenly burst into tears. As she cried, she said, "They never wanted me—I know that they hated the sight of me. I couldn't do anything, I couldn't say anything. Any time I asked a question mother told me to shut up."

Helen wept for almost an hour—with big, painful-sounding sobs at first, later with her tears flowing freely. As she wept she reviewed all the ways in which her parents had shut her up, rejected her, deprived her of the necessary feelings of being loved and wanted. A lifetime of sorrow and resentment was brought out.

At the end of the session she suddenly said, "Why, I can breathe! My nose is perfectly free—it's not plugged up at all!"

With the release of her tears there seemed to be a simultaneous release in her sinuses. Now, when she feels that her sinuses are plugging up, she has learned how to look for some repression which might have triggered the condition. When she finds a possible explanation, she takes some sort of action to overcome the repression—and her sinuses trouble her much less.

Perhaps by this time you have noticed that Helen began to get better after she cried, and you will recall that crying has been mentioned in connection with other patients. Perhaps you are wondering about the relationship between crying and successful psychotherapy, so a few words on the subject might not be amiss.

Is crying necessary for the treatment of a neurosis? Will a person get better if he cries? We don't think so. We notice that patients have two different types of crying: one, the sort of crying that is habitual, a response to frustration, a means of getting one's own way, or of making another person feel sorry. The other type of crying comes with deep sobs, at some profound realization of loss. A person can cry a bucket full of the first kind of tears without any apparent benefit; the second type of crying, however, usually indicates that the person's outlook on life will begin to get happier.

Certain emotions, especially those connected with loss of someone dearly loved, seem to be best released by crying. If the tears are held back, they find an outlet somewhere—but that outlet might be in an illness. When the dammed-up tears are finally shed, the illness is less necessary.

HAY FEVER

The things which have been said about the common cold and sinus trouble can also be said about hay fever—that it may be a non-verbal communication, that it may be an attempt to express some emotion. That it is a re-play of a behavior pattern which was successful at an earlier date, and so on.

If we suggest this to a patient, however, we usually meet with this objection: "But hay fever is caused by an allergy—I'm sensitive to rag-weed pollen. I've had skin tests and they *prove* it."

Very true—but remember that this book is not concerned with denying previous explanations for disease; instead we are trying to suggest other additional explanations. Rag-weed pollen can produce the symptoms of hay fever in an allergic person—but possibly there are other explanations besides.

There is the classical story of the man who was sensitive to roses. Whenever he was around roses, his nose would start to run, he would begin to sneeze, and he would develop all the symptoms of what the medical profession calls hyperesthetic rhinitis (a sensitive, irritated nose). One day this man went into his doctor's office and saw a beautiful rose in a bud-vase on the desk—and his symptoms began promptly and dramatically. Then the doctor showed him that it was an *artificial* rose, incapable of producing pollen or any other nasal irritants. The man thereupon recognized that it wasn't roses to which he reacted; instead, it was *his idea* of roses.

Here's another consideration: in medicine we classify disease-producing factors into three types—the predisposing, the precipitating and the perpetuating. The predisposing factors make one susceptible to a disease, or they lower one's resistance to a disease; the precipitating factors are those which bring the disease into activity; the perpetuating factors are those which tend to keep the disease plugging along without healing.

In hay fever and other allergic conditions it may well be that the pollens, the molds, the foods to which the person is sensitive all act as precipitating factors. But consider that there might be predisposing factors, such as severe emotional upsets, which put the patient into such a state that he acts as if he had no choice but to have hay fever. These emotion-laden fixed relationships may also keep the disease activated much longer than the patient wishes.

There was the case of Joe, a handsome eighteen-year-old

boy who had had hay fever since childhood. It wasn't actually disabling—he didn't have to go to a hay fever resort to obtain relief—but it was sufficient to keep him out of many activities which he said he liked. He couldn't go out for football, for instance—but it was noticeable that he could become the manager of the football team, a job which exposed him to as much pollen as he would get if he were playing. But by being the manager he didn't have to come into rough bodily contact with his team-mates and opponents; he could sit on the sidelines and sniffle in comfort and safety.

In therapy he was assisted to an awareness of the sorts of situations which made his hay fever worse—or at least that was the way he expressed it at the start. He learned, however, to say, "I get into such-and-such a situation and my hay fever symptoms become more pronounced." In other words, he learned to be aware of his choosing to have hay fever under certain circumstances—not that the circumstances *forced* him to get hay fever.

It came out that his mother was over-solicitous, overly anxious that her little boy should be good, quiet, liked by everyone, inoffensive, kind, considerate and so on. In other words, she did her utmost to force Joe into a behavior-pattern in which his normal aggressiveness was completely repressed.

It can be seen so often that it is impossible to completely repress any emotion; if the emotion does not come out in the usual forms of activity, it will sneak out by some devious route. Joe wasn't permitted to express any aggression, especially toward his mother. But the aggression was there, nonetheless—and he "got even" with her by having hay fever and giving her something to worry about.

He also tried to maintain his own self-integrity by rejecting everything his mother told him. We have discussed previously how the various functions of the body seem to work in parallel with each other. Here was Joe rejecting his mother's words to the best of his frustrated abilities—and it was as if he had made his mother's irritating words equal to the irritating pollen of rag-weed. Instead of trying to get rid of the effects of the words, he tried to get rid of their equivalent, the pollen—so he sneezed to expel it from his nose, his eyes watered to expel it from this organ, he built up a thick wall of nasal mucus to protect himself from the irritation.

In the "how" part of his therapy he became aware of the manner in which he produced these symptoms, and he became acquainted with the repressed feelings of rage which accompanied his attacks. Then he was taught how he could express this rage in bodily activity: he learned how to get mad. When he learned how to get mad, as well as how not to get mad, it was as if he could choose between the two. He no longer had to dam up his channels of anger expression so that the rage could come out only through his nose—and his hay fever decreased considerably.

He was also helped to make an explanation of the "why" of his hay fever, which he did in numerous ways by considering past experiences which were related to his symptoms. The realization that those times were not the present time, that that reaction was not the only possible reaction and that he could differentiate and choose between times and reactions was also a factor in his recovery from hay fever.

OTHER RESPIRATORY DISEASES

It is the belief of most practioners of psychosomatic medicine that *all* diseases have some so-called psychogenic aspects. And why not? If we regard the mind as the function of the structure called the body, it follows that any change in function is, in a sense, a mental change. It isn't far-fetched, then, to regard some of the diseases which have a known cause—a "physical" cause, as it is usually expressed—as being amenable to psychotherapeutic methods.

Take tuberculosis, for example. It is a well-known fact that a certain type of micro-organism, the *Mycobacterium tuberculosis*, is always found in the disease we call tuberculosis; in fact, if we don't find the bacteria, we don't make that diagnosis. But there are many, many questions which can be asked, instead of just saying that the germ causes the disease and letting it go at that.

Why should one person get TB and another person, similarly exposed, remain healthy? Or why should a person get TB instead of asthma, hay fever or sinus trouble? And why should it take so long for a person to change from the state of having TB to that of not having TB? We can't answer these questions by talking about "lowered resistance" or "increased susceptibility" either, because these are only

131

labels which repeat the question—although they do succeed in concealing the question more effectively.

The psychosomatic viewpoint would say, "Maybe the precipitating factor in tuberculosis is a bacillus—but how about the predisposing and the perpetuating factors? Couldn't they be the results of experiences which necessarily involved both the psyche and the soma—that is, psychosomatic?"

Here's the case of Dora, a lovely young lady who had had tuberculosis for five years. She had spent a year in a sanitarium and had been treated by bed-rest and pneumothorax —the procedure in which air is injected into the space between the lung and the chest cavity, thereby collapsing the lung. Her case was, at the time she began psychotherapy, of the type called "arrested"—she no longer had a fever, the tuberculosis process was no longer progressive, and she had no tubercle bacilli in her sputum. She was still getting pneumothorax and was trying to follow the advice of plenty of rest, the minimum of activity and so on.

One of the first things her therapist noticed was that she had a peculiar breathing pattern; the movements of her chest were very restricted and there was evidence of considerable muscular tension in the diaphragm. She was also "nervous," shaky and had the wide-opened eyes which are associated with fear. In short, she was a typical picture of anxiety.

The first step in therapy was to let her find out that she could breathe differently, that it was not necessary to breathe always as if she were frightened. Along with this

132

went an investigation of the situations in which she was fearful—and one of her discoveries was that she was afraid of emotions; most of all she was afraid of fear! She was so afraid of being afraid that she was in a constant state of fear lest she would act fearful. She covered up her timidity quite well; she was often outspoken and insulting. She belittled her friends whenever she had the chance, and superficially seemed courageous. It was a false front which she presented to the world; behind it all was a very frightened girl.

She was taught how to be afraid—how to act *as if* she were fearful—and she found out that fear has a purpose. She learned that all of us, when confronted with situations which are potentially dangerous, become prepared to cope with this predicted danger. Our adrenal glands start working in such a way that we become more efficient runners or fighters—and there are times when it is vitally necessary to be so prepared. *Every* situation is not dangerous, however, and when we act as if we must be in constant readiness to flee or fight, we are not living as efficiently as we might.

When she learned how to become afraid she also learned how *not* to be afraid; she learned how to manage fear. She discovered that she could use fear when it was necessary, and not be forced to become fearful when it was unnecessary.

It was also demonstrated to her that she was afraid of her own anger. She had had numerous experiences wherein it was forcibly shown that anger always meets with punishment—so, in order to avoid punishment, she avoided anger.

In a certain sense, unexpressed or repressed anger is quite similar to fear—so she became fearful, breathed as one does during fear-states, and created a hospitable fertile condition in her lungs for any stray tubercle bacillus which was looking for a home.

Of course, her therapy included many other approaches in addition to this instruction in the management of her own emotions, but this was the essential part. Within three months she was enrolled in a school of drama, taking part in all the class activities, including interpretive dancing, and was able to do all this without any shortness of breath or fatigue. Ordinarily such an increase in activities would be almost fatal for a TB patient—but she seemed to thrive on it.

This case illustrates how a disease is not only the response to infection—it is also *a way of living*. And by changing one's patterns of living one can also change the course of the disease!

In addition to specific diseases of the respiratory system, we often see chronic behavior patterns which don't seem to have any particular cause. The most common of these is a frequently-repeated cough or a throat-clearing. You have seen people who use one of the little respiratory mannerisms as a form of punctuation—the deprecatory cough which follows the making of a controversial statement, the throat-clearing which announces that an emotionally-charged statement is about to be made, or the cough which is used for purposes of interruption.

There is another way of looking at these mannerisms; perhaps you will find it interesting. We have mentioned before that the various functions of the body work analogously with each other; one function parallels another. For example, when a person becomes angry he seems to become generally tense—his jaw muscles tighten, the muscles around his eyes contract to produce a frown, his hand and forearm muscles close to produce a clenched fist, the muscles of his chest and diaphragm become tense so that he holds his breath; even the muscles of his intestine become tense. In the act of rejection we see that a person tends to carry out this casting-out process with every possible function: his arms want to push away, he squints his eyes as if to reject the visualization of what he doesn't want to accept. The intestinal tract can take part in this, too; the mouth can reject by spitting out; the stomach can reject by nausea and vomiting; the colon can reject by diarrhea. In rejection there is a reversal of the inward flow and a speeding up of the outward flow.

In rejection by the respiratory system we can see a running nose, an exhalation of breath, a clearing of mucus from the throat or a cough—again, functions which expel an unwanted substance.

It should not be surprising to note that people will reject ideas as if they were substances—and we can see this process going on all the time. If a woman is quarrelling with her boy-friend and wants to reject him, she says, "You make me sick to my stomach. You're disgusting!" It is as if to say, "I am rejecting you from my digestive system because I can't tolerate you." Then she might cry, washing the sight of him out of her eyes and, within the next few days after this emotional upheaval, develop a cold in order to flush him out of her being via the mucus from the respiratory tract.

This particular viewpoint is brought up here because of its interest rather than to make the claim that it is absolutely and incontrovertibly so. It is possible to find exceptions to this explanation of body-function—it is, nonetheless, an interpretation of certain mannerisms which are difficult to explain in any other way.

It can be helpful, however, in increasing one's own self-awareness. If you have a chronic cough, or frequent nausea, or recurring attacks of diarrhea, you might try to figure out whether you're trying to reject something, and, if so, what? You can recognize then that you can refuse to accept an idea without dragging the whole body in on the act. You don't have to confuse an intangible idea with mucus to be coughed out or food to be vomited out or excreta to be defecated out—or even with the contents of the uterus to be menstruated out!

DISEASES OF THE GASTRO-INTESTINAL SYSTEM

Among those doctors who keep in mind that the human organism works as a whole there is no disagreement that the intestinal tract reflects the function of the whole person. Everybody knows this; they know it so well that they frequently lose sight of it. Every mother knows that a baby who has an emotionally-upsetting experience is apt to get an upset stomach. Everybody has seen unpleasant sights which make them swallow hard to prevent the waves of nausea from becoming outright vomiting. Everyone knows that fear can tie your stomach up in knots, that excitement can give you "butterflies in the belly," that sorrow can make you lose your appetite.

It is when these functional disorders go on so long that they result in structural changes that some people—and a lot of doctors, too—seem to forget that there is still an emotional component to the illness. In focussing on the structural change they overlook the functional changes which brought it about and prevent it from healing. When the doctor sees an X-ray picture which reveals a definite ulcer crater, he tends to treat the ulcer, rather than the patient— and the countless numbers of recurrent ulcers, unhealed ulcers and complications of ulcer testify that medical attention must not be confined to one small area of the mucous membrane of the stomach.

What happens when a person develops a peptic ulcer? (We use the term "peptic" ulcer to refer to ulcers which are in the pepsin-producing region in the lower part of the stomach and the first part of the small intestine.) Numerous things happen with various causes and effects, with one effect being a cause for another effect. We notice that the stomach acts as if it were constantly hungry or, in other cases, as if constantly full of food. In both these states there is an increased secretion of hydrochloric acid by the cells of the gastric mucosa; other digestive juices are poured out, and the muscles of the stomach move as if food were being churned and digested.

But peptic ulcer is *not* just a disease of the peptic area:

the whole person is involved. We can expect to find—and we do find—a rather characteristic personality pattern to go along with the pattern of the ulcer. The typical ulcer patient tends to be a worrier; he is often aggressive and competent, the type of individual who becomes a high-pressure salesman, or an account executive in an advertising firm, or a program director in a radio station, or a doctor. We find the ulcer's host in a position where he has earned the right to have great responsibilities—and it is almost as if he acquired these responsibilities in order to have something more to worry about.

Behind this facade of mature energy and responsibility we see evidences of the exact opposite of this. When the ulcer patient's defenses are down, he tends to become a little boy again, dependent on the direction of his superiors, anxious for love and affection and tender care.

It is interesting to observe the parallelism between the symptoms and treatment of ulcer and the behavior pattern of an infant. The infant takes small, frequent feedings; so does the ulcer patient. The infant becomes hungry about every four hours; so does the ulcer patient. The infant complains bitterly and querulously when he doesn't have his hunger-wants attended to; did you ever see an ulcer patient who was frustrated? Petulant whining seems to be the favorite response, with anger being a close second. What do they feed babies, and what do they feed ulcer patients? Milk and strained foods, of course.

We suspect that this peculiar conflict, the desire to be an infant and a mature individual simultaneously, is one of

138

the important factors in the development of peptic ulcer. It is as if he remained an infant in his stomach functions and proceeded to be an adult in his other functions. He can tolerate this state of partial adulthood for just so long—then his ulcer kicks up and he must revert to the infantile pattern of behavior where he is put to bed, fed frequently with soft foods which don't need chewing and has sympathy and attention lavished upon him. Then, after playing baby for a while, he recovers, and is able to return to an adult behavior pattern.

Now, of course, this isn't the only way that we can speak about an ulcer patient or the process of formation and treatment of peptic ulcers. Each school of psychiatric thought has its own viewpoint; the Freudians, for example, speak of fixation of the libido at the oral-receptive, oral-aggressive levels, and of guilt-feelings over the social oral-aggressiveness. By using this viewpoint and the appropriate psychiatric or psychoanalytic approach, many patients have been helped.

But there is also a slightly different viewpoint and a slightly different therapeutic approach, which we can best discuss by talking about Roger. Roger was in his middle thirties, a successful junior editor on a national magazine. It was a position which required a lot of aggressiveness, initiative and drive—and Roger had these qualities. At least he had them at work—but at home it was a different matter. At the time he came in for therapy he had been married and divorced twice and was about to remarry for the third time. Apropos of this he remarked ruefully, "I have to have a good position and a good salary so that I can pay all the alimony my ex-wives stuck me with."

In discussing the probable reasons for his divorces he remarked that his two unsuccessful marriages were marked by misunderstandings and by quarrels. When he got married, he expected that his bride would be sweet, affectionate and understanding—but when the honeymoon was over, she became nagging and domineering—"It was enough to drive a man crazy."

Now in such cases, it often helps to ask this question: "Suppose that you *wanted* your wife to act in the way she did, how would you go about making her act that way?" The usual response—and Roger's response, too—is for the patient to say, "Why should I want to make my wife nag me? That's silly."

"But just supposing that you deliberately and maliciously set out to make your wife nag you, how could you do it?"

"Well, I'd act childish, and I'd put off doing the things she asked me to do, and I'd be forgetful about messages for her—say, I *did* do all those things! Do you mean to say that I wanted her to nag me?"

To this the therapist made no reply, but countered with another question: "Who used to nag you when you were a little boy?"

"My mother. Hmmm." And with that the process of increased self-awareness got under way.

It was demonstrated to Roger—and he did the demonstrating, of course—that among his many behavior patterns he had two which stood out with considerable distinctness.

One pattern was the one he used in business—manly, mature, aggressive, driving. The other was the pattern he used around women, especially around his former wives and his current fiancée; in this he was dependent, childish, attention-seeking, demanding of food, talking, kissing and other mouth-centered activities. He became aware of the various gestures, mannerisms, bodily attitudes and feeling states which composed these two patterns.

The therapist used this analogy: "Supposing that a man had two rooms that he could go into, and that he couldn't decide which one to stay in. He would go into one room, take a quick look around, go into the other, then back to the first and so on. He would spend so much time vacillating from one to the other that he wouldn't find out what either room was suited for. Now, what else can he do? He can go into one room and explore it thoroughly, finding out what the advantages and disadvantages of this room are. Then he can go into the other room and repeat the process. After this, he can decide what room to go into under what circumstances; he can choose to enter the room most suited to the time of day, his current needs, and so on. Now—let's consider these behavior patterns of yours as if they were rooms and find out what each of them is good for."

So Roger was given the chance to practice the act of being an infant to the fullest extent—not just with his stomach and intestinal tract. He learned again how to cry like a baby, how to feel weak and helpless like a baby, how to feel resentful at being treated like a baby. Then he practiced at being a mature man, accepting completely the responsibilities for which he was hungry and how to assimilate them into his total being. His ulcer gradually ceased to trouble him, and within a few months the X-ray showed that it had healed. Since then, he has had numerous opportunities for developing ulcer symptoms again, but he has been able to choose not to have them.

Is he cured? Who can say? Perhaps observation for another ten years would enable one to give a more definite answer. At present all that can be said is that his present personality structure does not go with the development of peptic ulcer; Roger has changed sufficiently so that the possibilities of the ulcer's recurring are becoming quite remote. This particular approach to the ulcer problem—or to any psychosomatic disease for that matter—is still a little too new to be fully evaluated. And note that we don't say that it's a *different* method so much as that it's *another* method. We're dealing with the same old subject—the human mind as it works in the body—and we've known about the existence of that for centuries.

Anything as complex as a human being can be viewed from many, many diverse aspects—all of which can be partially correct, none of which is completely correct. We are suggesting for consideration another point of view; it may be a "mistake," as discussed before, but you know how necessary a mistake can be.

Just for the fun of it we're going to make a list of all the disorders seen in the digestive tract which might be of psychosomatic origin or which may have emotional components. Here goes: chapped lips, decayed teeth, sore gums, bleeding gums, sore tongue, excessive salivation, insufficient salivation, halitosis, tonsillitis, pharyngitis, "sore throat," difficulty in swallowing, compulsive swallowing, cardiospasm (the condition in which the muscle guarding the entrance to the stomach fails to open up), nausea, vomiting, "heart-burn"—but that's enough. Notice how many possibilities have been mentioned, and we still haven't gone beyond the first part of the stomach. But they are there, and many more besides, until we finally get to colitis, constipation, hemorrhoids and anal fissures.

Let us consider the various functions of the digestive tract, and discuss some of the relationships of these functions to other bodily functions and to the body-as-a-whole. Perhaps we can understand more about it if we consider the most primitive aspects of this function. We can think of a living being—a simple one-celled animal or a complex human—as a biochemical device for absorbing what it requires from its environment, using a part of what it absorbs for acquiring energy, discarding what it does not need. In the one-celled animal like the amoeba or the paramecium, the one cell accomplishes all the functions, plus other functions such as motility and reproduction. As we ascend the evolutionary scale and observe more complex animals, we see that specific phases of these functions of absorption, assimilation and excretion are taken over by certain organs. The lungs specialize in the absorption and excretion of gases; the blood specializes in the task of distributing absorbed air and absorbed nourishment; the nervous system specializes in the absorption, assimilation and excretion of information about the raw material with which the intestines, the lungs and the sex organs deal.

In the more complex vertebrate animals the acquisition of energy may be a passive process or an active process; when the energy is easily available, the animal doesn't have to fight for it.

And so it goes with food; when the food is simply poured into his digestive tract, he can be passively receptive. When food is scarce, he needs to go out and find it, fight for it, overcome it and devour it. For this he needs weapons—teeth to cut off pieces of this energy-giving environment, molars to grind it into swallowable bits, digestive enzymes which can break it down further into assimilable chemicals and, finally, a system for expelling the unutilizable residue.

The digestive function is, therefore, one—but *not* the only one—of the primitive functions which go to make up the process of living and surviving. Other more complex processes go along with it, paralleling its function, abetting its function, inter-relating with its function.

Primitive functions, like primitive people, can be easily influenced and changed by more complexly evolved functions. The complex functions of emotion can and do influence the primitive function of digestion; the highly complex function called thinking can influence it even more, both for better and for worse. But the primitive functions can also influence the more complex ones—and this inter-relationship gives us a chance to manipulate and produce the changes we call therapy.

There are certain behavior patterns, loosely grouped

under the heading of "neurosis," which have intestinal counterparts. It is difficult to re-train the more complex behavior patterns, much easier to re-train the primitive behavior patterns.

Suppose that a person is weak, ineffectual, unaggressive, a passive receiver of all statements which are sent in his direction. We shall usually find that that person manifests the same sort of intestinal function. He prefers soft, practically pre-chewed and pre-digested foods; he has weak, decaying teeth; his jaw muscles are as flabby as his personality. When he puts food into his mouth, he tends to gum it and gulp it without macerating it into tiny digestible particles. On the "intellectual" level he swallows all sorts of information without tasting it to determine its edibility, especially if it's sugar-coated and accompanied by the assurance, "This is good for you, darling—it will make you nice and strong."

It has been seen in numerous experiments that if this person learns to act more forcefully toward his food, it will be much easier for him to act more aggressively toward the remainder of his environment. By a deliberate process of self-training, aided by the encouragement of a good therapist, a person can re-learn to use his intestinal tract as an instrument for making his environment a part of himself. He can learn to *bite* off a chunk of hard, chewy bread. His usual technique has probably been to worry it off, or instead, to use his teeth only to hold, while he tore off the bread with his hand. Then he can learn to chew his food thoroughly and completely, with his attention directed at the process of chewing and all it entails, instead of diverting his attention with reading the newspaper or nagging his children. He can maintain an awareness of the sensations of taste, of the touch sensation of the gradually liquefying food, of the zestful interaction between strong jaw muscles and resistant food. He can learn to recognize his food likes and what they can imply; does he want a tough, resistive manly steak or does he want milk and infant foods or the ice cream and sweets which are the reward for being a good little boy?

Much of this work of re-training primitive functions as a means of altering a neurotic behavior pattern is still in the experimental stage. There is still not enough information to be able to say that Caspar Milquetoast can become a prize-fighter simply by learning how to chew aggressively. In a number of cases observed, however, considerable benefits have been seen without any appearance of harmful effects.

We might also mention the re-training of the lower end of the intestinal tract, the part whose function is to expel the residue of food which can't be used. When this function is disturbed, we usually see one of two extremes: constipation or diarrhea.

Let's consider a disease in which there is a disturbance of elimination, with the disturbance being on the side of over-activity. A good example of that is *colitis*, in which there is an inflammation of the large intestine. One of the results of this condition is that the patient has frequent, painful, bloody stools; he has the extreme in diarrhea.

It is possible for a person with this highly uncomfortable

146

condition to re-train his intestinal tract so that he doesn't have to move his bowels so frequently. One way to do it is to observe all the sensations which go along with the rush directed toward the toilet. What are the sensations? Where do they start? What is the emotion which accompanies the urge to defecate—anger at having to go? Fear of another painful bowel movement? Sorrow at being in this state of ill-health? What disturbing experience preceded the episode?

Asking this sort of question will sometimes give the person a clue to what he is doing. One patient, for example, said that he felt as if he were trying to get rid of something bad. With further thinking along these lines, he concluded that he was trying to get rid of his mother's over-solicitude and "smother love." As he recognized that there were other ways to get rid of this besides trying to defecate it out, the symptoms subsided.

Yes, we can see some rather startling changes when we don't take for granted the functioning of our bodies, when we ask questions and try to experiment with changing our habitual behavior-patterns. Here is another example of how changing food-functions can lead to better health. George was one of those men who wasn't quite sure of what he wanted; he was reasonably successful, but he wasn't sure that he was being successful in the most successful way. He was happily married, but still preoccupied with extra-marital affairs. It was noticed that he had a strong drive toward making things—he made furniture, he made music, and he frequently referred to his sexual escapades as "making a girl." He spoke about the problem of how he *made* his children obey him and how he made his customers buy his products.

It was suggested to George that he refrain from eating until he was definitely certain of what he wanted. The experiment started after the noon lunch; he reported no especial hunger at dinner-time. When he went to bed that night, he thought he was hungry, and thought a lot about food—then he suddenly realized that he was thinking about *making* something to eat. With that he went to sleep. It was not until the following afternoon that he recognized what he wanted—a good, tasty, chewy steak—and he ate it with more relish and enjoyment than any meal he had had in months. This and other experiments at which he has plugged away have helped George to be more certain of what he wants; he is less interested in having extra-marital affairs, for one thing, and he also reports that he doesn't feel compelled to spend so much time in his work-shop.

Coincidence? Perhaps—but at any rate it's an interesting experiment. You might like to try it.

You can ask the same questions about constipation; first consider what primitive function we accomplish by having a bowel movement, then think of the more complex functions which parallel this.

Of course, you can't always get an answer by asking such questions. Not infrequently the confusion in a person's mind is so profound that it might take years to unravel the tangled skein of associations. But we have found—and we think that you will find, too—that you stand a better chance of getting an answer when you ask a question than if you suffer in silence.

GLANDULAR DISEASES

There is another group of illnesses with which psychosomatic medicine deals—the glandular diseases. In this group we place those conditions in which there is an upset in the function of the endocrine (or ductless) glands. Examples of such diseases would include obesity, toxic goiter, menstrual difficulties and sexual under-development. This is not a complete list by any means, but the discussion of a few of these conditions will show what psychosomatic medicine has to offer, both in explanation and in treatment.

The endocrine glands, as we said before, are the glands whose secretions (hormones) go directly into the bloodstream. The hormones act as chemical messengers, preparing the body-as-a-whole for emergency situations. We believe that certain sensations result when there is a sudden change in the amount of any hormone in the blood, and we call these sensations emotions.

It has been conclusively shown that any emotional stress, such as being kept in a constant state of fear or anger, will produce definite changes in some of the endocrine glands; in time these changes can be found in other organs, such as the sex glands, the kidneys and the intestines. These changes can be produced by any one of a number of conditions, including exposure to cold, burning, poisoning, injury, even by over-doses of other hormones.

We don't intend to give you a complete course in endocrinology; the subject is too complicated and too fascinating to be squeezed into a book of this size. It should be enough to say that the endocrine glands seem to function in such a way as to enable us to cope better with emergencies, to enable us to respond to stress in a more effective manner; in addition to this they are vitally concerned with the development and maintenance of the reproductive functions, and, of course, they are intimately concerned with the process of growth.

There is a more subtle, probably more important function than these, which also seems to go along with endocrine and emotional changes: the ability to evaluate. It seems that the ability to say and think and feel that one thing is better than another or worse than another is based on the functioning of the endocrine glands.

Imagine making a list of all the evaluations which are possible to you. At the top would be those actions which you think will keep you alive in the longest, happiest manner possible; at the bottom of the list would be those things which would cause sudden, immediate death. All the rest of your actions and beliefs would be arranged somewhere between these two extremes.

It is our impression that location on this list is determined by the emotion (i.e., the hormone level) which is associated with it. When we love someone, we value him highly and we have a certain hormone-response to him; when we hate him, we have another hormone pattern associated with him. A person who doesn't love or hate is one whose endocrine system is not working properly.

We could start an argument that would last for a long time by saying that loving makes the glandular system function. Somebody else could take the opposite view, that the function or certain endocrine glands makes a person feel like loving—and we'd both be correct. Let's side-step this argument by saying that the two functions, glandular and evaluative, work together.

This point is brought up at this time to make it a little more clear that an emotional change goes along with a glandular change, which goes along with a bodily change. It's another example of how impossible it is to separate the "mind" and the "body."

But enough of this theorizing. Let's talk about one of the problems of glandular dysfunction: obesity. We say that obesity is a glandular problem, and that's true—but not entirely. We know that metabolism (the process of getting energy from our food) is controlled by various ductless glands: when the thyroid works overtime, the person loses weight in spite of the amount he eats; a person with a disorder of the pituitary gland may either gain or lose weight tremendously.

Offhand, it might seem that all we would have to do to help an obese person lose weight would be to give him enough of the proper hormone. Sometimes it works that way—but oftener it does not.

This was illustrated in the case of Corinne. She had been a fat baby, a plump little girl, and now, at the age of twenty-six, she was still obese. She had a round, baby face, with lovely smooth skin; it was a pretty face, but the body which was attached to it was grotesque. Her upper arms were huge; her thighs were massive; her breasts, abdomen and buttocks were gigantic.

She was, as might be expected, an enormous eater. Not only did she have three large meals every day, but she also loved to have an ice-cream soda in the morning and a nice thick malted milk in the middle of the afternoon. A bed-time snack was routine, too—and in between times Corinne fortified herself with chocolate bars.

When she was asked why she ate so much, she replied, "Well, doctor, I really don't want to eat so much—but I get so darned hungry. If I missed a meal, I'd get so weak that I'd just collapse."

Needless to say, Corinne wasn't very happy. She had the jovial personality which is usually associated with obesity; she laughed easily and frequently, and made a lot of wise-cracks—but there was an air of quiet desperation behind all this. It didn't take long before she poured out her troubles: "I don't want to be fat. Nobody loves a fat girl. I don't get invited to dances, I don't have any boy-friends. People seem to *like* me—but it never goes any further than liking. It looks as if I'm doomed to be an old maid."

That seemed to be one clue to her difficulties—a fear of not having those things which marriage can supply. She was afraid that she wouldn't be loved, wouldn't have sexual gratification, wouldn't have children, wouldn't have com-panionship. At the same time, as so often happens with fears, she was also afraid of what having these things might involve.

152

As she gradually recognized this confusion in her desires, she began to see how eating was a substitute for other actions: whenever she was happy, whenever she was sad, whenever she was frustrated, instead of taking the action which would express her emotions or which would solve her problems, she would eat. And when she was anxious, eating seemed to keep her from feeling quite so frightened.

This fixed pattern of response dated from childhood, she believed. She recalled how much stress was placed on eating "good, nourishing foods," how frequently she was rewarded for "being good" by being given sweets; in fact, "being good" and eating were practically the same thing.

There was also a confusion between eating and being strong; she had been taught that food was strengthening, that she *had* to eat or she wouldn't grow up to be a big, strong girl. She recognized that she needed strength in order to conquer her obesity; that meant that the way to lose weight was to grow fat. When this highly irrational way of thinking was uncovered, she went into gales of laughter—at the absurdity of it.

As Corinne learned to take actions other than eating, as she found out that she could have other pleasant sensations besides a full stomach, as she recognized that she didn't have to stick to the values of eating which were given to her in childhood, she gradually became thinner. It helped also to recognize that food was something which could be chewed and tasted, not just stomach-stuffing.

Was Corinne's trouble glandular? There was certainly an element of glandular difficulty there; but the imbalance of hormones seemed to depend on emotions and evaluations. When she changed these, she was able to change her pattern of over-eating. Once again the mistake in the early learning pattern could be corrected and a more satisfying behavior learned.

She could have been treated in many other ways besides this; she could have been given hormones, and medicines to reduce her appetite; she could have been placed on a rigid diet and starved to thinness. Without a knowledge of the basic reasons for obesity, however, these methods are exceedingly difficult, often ineffective, and relapse is frequent.

It's a safe generalization to say that glandular difficulties and emotional difficulties go hand in hand; results can be obtained by treating either. Better results are obtained by treating both.

Here's another case which illustrates the inter-relationship between endocrine function and emotion: Dorothy was an attractive young woman who had been married five years. She and her husband were not getting along too well, especially when it came to having marital relations. Dorothy's religious training forbade her to be divorced, and it also included the teaching that a wife must not deny her husband his "marital rights."

She was in a quandary; she didn't want to have intercourse with her husband, yet she was not permitted to refuse him.

Her husband had a job which took him out of the city at irregular intervals and for irregular periods of time. No matter how long he had been gone, and no matter when her previous menstrual period had occurred, she would begin to menstruate within two or three hours of his return home. It seemed as if her glandular system had solved the problem of how not to have intercourse, for both she and her husband regarded menstruation as a definite barrier to sexual relations. (This is not so; the objections to intercourse during menstruation are esthetic, not physiologic.)

It requires a decidedly profound change of glandular function to menstruate as irregularly as she did. The normal hormonal pattern which controls menstruation is a series of cyclic changes, repeating every twenty-eight days; Dorothy had altered her cycle to menstruate as often as she could to prevent her having intercourse.

She had consulted an endocrinologist for her menstrual difficulties. She didn't mention her emotional problem to him, as she was not aware that her difficulties might include an emotional factor. The physician tried valiantly to adjust her menstrual cycle by giving her a plentiful supply of the proper hormones at the proper time. She improved for a couple of months, then her difficulties recurred—only this time she started to menstruate and continued without stopping.

At the advice of friends, she consulted a doctor who was interested in psychosomatic medicine. Dorothy quickly discovered that there was a definite pattern of mood changes which accompanied her menstrual irregularity; when she was not menstruating, she was tense and apprehensive, and when her period began, she would feel relaxed and triumphant. She considered the idea that she might dislike her husband, which she rejected, because she felt that she was sincerely in love with him.

As her therapy progressed, she became aware that she didn't like to have intercourse. Her therapist made this suggestion: "Here are two statements—'I don't like' and 'to have intercourse.' Notice that this statement shows a problem that can be solved in two ways—by not having intercourse or by changing the 'not liking' part of it. You've tried to solve it by not having intercourse, and look what's happened. Let's try to find out *why* you don't like it."

Within a short time Dorothy had recalled all the evaluations of sex which had been forced on her by her well-intentioned mother. She also learned how to become aware of the sensations which make up the experience of making love. By comparing the actual sensations with the words which had been applied to the sensations, she came to the conclusion that she would rather accept her own sensations than another person's evaluation. Within a few months her menses became regular and her marital life became a joy, not a problem.

This case illustrates a viewpoint which has been found to be valuable. It can be expressed as a question: what is the purpose of disease? If we regard disease as something mysterious caused entirely by external forces, we are led to conclude that disease is something out of our control. We become choiceless, helpless and, once in a while, hopeless.

If, on the other hand, we consider that every disease has been purposive, if we assume that the person is becoming ill in an attempt to survive better, if we regard "illness" as a mistaken form of "health," then we are no longer powerless. There is some sort of action we can take, if only the action of searching for a cause. And we know that action is closer to health than is inaction.

While we are discussing glandular diseases, we might also mention the endocrine aspects of homosexuality.

In the case of male homosexuality we see a person who is acting like a woman, but with a male body; with female homosexuality the reverse is true. One is tempted to jump to the conclusion that this is due to an over-supply of hormones of the opposite sex, and that the obvious treatment is to increase the supply of hormones of the structural sex. In other words, to a male homosexual we should give a lot of male hormones, which will make him cease acting like a female.

Sad to say, this isn't so. It has been tried numerous times, and the chief result seems to be an exaggeration of the already existing pattern. The male homosexual who is given male hormones becomes more aggressively homosexual; the hormone has increased his aggressiveness, but hasn't altered the direction of his sex-drive.

Successful treatment of homosexuality is based on helping the patient to an understanding of *how* he acts, in order to play the role of the opposite sex, and *why* he chooses to act that way. We would not look for *the* reason for his being a homosexual, but for the many, many reasons which might make this sort of behavior the least worse method of sur viving.

So far we have talked about those glandular diseases wherein there is an under-supply of certain hormones. There is such a thing as an over-supply, too—and a typical example of that is the condition known as thyrotoxicosis, or toxic goiter, or exophthalmic goiter.

The most prominent feature of this condition is the eyes, which look as if they were about to pop out of the head. That's what the Greek word "exophthalmic" means—the eyes are out. With this unsightly condition of the eyes, we also observe a fast pulse, increased breathing rate, a general speeding up of all the body functions. The patient usually has an enormous appetite, yet loses weight in spite of his increased food intake. He is apt to be nervous, irritable, easily excited; in the early stages of the disease he has a lot of pep and energy, but he later becomes easily exhausted.

The disease is said to be "caused" by an over-active thyroid gland, and the usual treatment is to give a drug which depresses thyroid function, or to remove a large portion of the gland.

Let us digress for a moment to discuss what happens when one speaks of a disease having "a cause"; if there is *a* cause—just *one* cause—for a disease, it follows that there is only one treatment. And if that treatment doesn't work too well, then where are you?

We can also see a tendency, when speaking of "a disease," to limit our relationships to that disease. In other words, when we talk about a toxic thyroid, we concern ourselves only with the various signs and symptoms which go to make up the picture of the condition. We thereby tend to ignore

158

relationships between the signs and symptoms and other conditions in the person's environment.

Sounds complicated, doesn't it? Let's give an example: if a doctor sees a person with prominent eyeballs, he thinks first of toxic goiter, and he looks for the other symptoms which go to make up that disease. If a psychosomaticist sees prominent eyeballs, he thinks of the reasons for having eyes which protrude; he asks such questions as: in what emotional state do a person's eyes protrude? During fear? During anger? During grief? During sexual excitement? Does this person act as if he were angry or fearful? If so, under what circumstances does he have these emotions? Are these circumstances commonly present in his every-day life? What experiences has this person had which might have taught him that the way to survive is to be pop-eyed?

In asking these questions, we open up the possibilities of making other relationships between the symptom and the rest of the person's life. We are not forced to conclude that the *only* way to treat thyrotoxicosis is to depress or excise the thyroid gland. And sometimes the patient is able to be spared the necessity for surgery.

Doris had a noticeable case of exophthalmic goiter. Her eyeballs were very prominent, so much so that you could see a narrow strip of white between the iris and the upper lid. She looked as if she were scared—and she acted the same way. She had a nervous, mirthless giggle at frequent intervals; there were times when she laughed without any apparent reason.

One of the first steps was to teach her how to "pop" her

159

eyes deliberately. She didn't think at first that it could be done—but some practice in front of a mirror showed that it was quite possible. She noticed that, as she learned how to produce this glassy stare, she did it much less frequently.

Next was an investigation of the circumstances which were apt to result in the pop-eyed state; she found that circumstances which "frightened" her or "made her mad" would usually result in her eyes protruding. She learned to differentiate between being *made* frightened or angry, and *becoming* frightened or angry. She became able to act angry or frightened deliberately and voluntarily, and, as she did so, to make her eyes stick out. With this increasing ability to have emotions at will, she became less of an unwilling victim of those people who, in her opinion "made" her have those responses. In other words, she learned how to choose her responses, and to make a response which was appropriate to the situation.

It wasn't too long before her condition improved to such an extent that an operation, once thought inevitable, was now unnecessary. Her eyes now are gradually receding; there will be an occasional flare-up when she is presented with a situation which she has not yet worked through, but these are becoming fewer. With this apparent change in the endocrine function of the thyroid have come changes in other endocrine functions: she had formerly taken estrogenic (ovarian) hormone in large doses, but now is able to discontinue the use of it entirely.

Another glandular condition which seems to fall into the category of psychosomatic illness is diabetes. Any sort of emotional stress is apt to show up in an increase in the amount of sugar in the blood-stream and in the urine. There is an urge to over-eat, and one of the early signs of diabetes is a rapid gain in weight.

As yet it is impossible to say that diabetes can be "cured" by psychotherapy; nevertheless, numerous cases have been reported in which there was a decrease in the severity of the symptoms. It would therefore seem like a good idea for every diabetic to consider psychotherapy as an additional way to work toward the greatest possible health.

THE SKIN

The question, "Why skin disease?" is one which is diffi-cult to answer. You can see that there might be difficulties in teaching a person how to have a skin disease as part of the process of teaching him how not to have it—but people *can* be taught to reproduce the sensations of an itchy or painful dermatitis. They may not be able to develop the skin lesions of eczema, but they can recall the sensation of it.

Here is a suggestion which might explain the mechanism of skin irritations: Let us assume that there was a time when a person had a sensation on a given part of his skin and at the same time he had perceptions of other sights, sounds, etc. Whenever these sights or sounds are experienced again, there is a tendency to associate them with the skin sensa-tion. If the person *must* have that sort of skin sensation, one way he can obtain it is to have some sort of skin eruption.

Here's another possibility: we mentioned before that every

one of us will respond emotionally to certain stimuli, and that we learn through experience to associate a stimulus with an emotional response. We have said also that the energy of emotions demands an outlet; if it cannot be discharged in some form of bodily activity, it will come out by less desirable channels.

How can we supply this principle to skin disease? We might consider the person who is chronically angry, who feels like a volcano on the verge of eruption. He has been taught that he shouldn't express his anger—and this dammed-up force finally breaks out through his skin. It is interesting to note that skin conditions are often referred to as "eruptions" and "breaking out"; could it be that our popular terminology is more accurate than we give it credit for?

This explanation seemed to apply to the case of Betty, who had developed a severe, burning moist irritation in the region at one time covered by a diaper. When asked to describe the skin condition, she said, "It looks so angry. It dries up for a while, then it starts weeping again. That's the only change it has made."

Closer questioning revealed that her husband had recently made a change in his job, over which she first became angry, then did a lot of weeping. With further discussion she modified that statement, saying that she felt angry, and felt like weeping, but didn't do anything about it because she felt that such expression of emotion was unbecoming to an adult.

The therapist asked her to think about her skin condition,

162

to feel it, and then act as if she were angry—to give vent to primitive, unrepressed rage. She did so for a few moments, then reported that her skin felt more comfortable than it had for days. She was then asked to pretend that she felt sad about her skin condition. "I don't have to pretend," was her answer. "I feel sad about it already."

"How does your skin feel now?"

"It's starting to itch again. Oh, why did you have to change it? It felt so good."

The therapist then suggested that she act as if she were crying. She did so, but in a very few moments the pretended weeping changed into actual tears and sobbing. When this outburst had subsided, she again reported that her skin felt comfortable.

It isn't often that one sees a person who responds as dramatically as Betty did. In her case the tie-up between her repressed emotions and her skin-expression of them was quite obvious. Nor was her skin completely healed as a result of this demonstration. It required numerous discussions of all possible relationships between the dermatitis and her every-day life.

MUSCULO-SKELETAL DISEASES

One of the still-unsolved medical mysteries is arthritis. Investigation into its causes and the search for effective means of treatment are the life-work of a great number of investigators. The drugs used in the treatment of arthritis form a list as long as your arm—and none of them are very effective except temporarily. The use of cortisone and

ACTH seems to be promising. The various types of arthritis have been classified and re-classified—but classification of disease, while interesting to the doctor, is not much help to the patient. The list of suggested causes is endless—bacteria, viruses, food deficiencies, vitamin deficiencies, glandular disturbances, "focal infection"—yet treatments aimed at altering these conditions do not work nearly as often as we would like.

The majority of arthritis-sufferers usually wind up by taking aspirin and having fortitude. They "learn to live with their disease." They try to console themselves with the thought that it might be worse, and they are taught to regard the halting of the process as a major victory.

Let's look at the arthritis-rheumatism group of diseases from another angle. Let's try to find out what one accomplishes by having arthritis.

In order to discuss it, consider an extreme case of what is called atrophic arthritis. We see that the joints of the body become shapeless masses of calcium deposits; the patient often loses the use of his hands, which become like flippers. Or the process may affect the spine, so that it becomes completely stiff, like a poker. Or it may affect the knees, so they swell up to two or three times normal size and become fixed and unbending.

To sum this up, we can say that the patient gets into a state where he can't move. And why should he do this?

A study of arthritis sufferers made at one of the Chicago hospitals shows that they have a rather characteristic behavior pattern. These people are apt to be hostile and aggressive, yet seem to be unable to express these feelings. During their childhood and youth they were usually extremely interested in competitive sports, but when the duties of adulthood prevented them from letting off steam in this way, the joint-stiffening process developed rapidly.

We might even say that the arthritis sufferer was afraid to show that he had feelings which would lead him to fight with others—and he became stiff in order to make certain that he wouldn't.

It must be said right here that we don't know whether or not psychotherapy can promise a cure in a full-blown case of arthritis. We don't know whether the stiffened joints can regain their full motion. We don't know whether the calcium deposits can be re-absorbed.

There has not been a sufficient amount of experience with the psychosomatic approach; however, in those cases which have been observed, a few definite trends were noticed. When these trends were dealt with according to the principles expressed in this book, it was noticeable that the patients experienced a relief from the severity of their troubles. We pass the observations on to you, not as a final definitive statement, but for your further consideration.

As we mentioned before, the characteristic point of arthritis is non-movement—and yet, we see that arthritis develops in energetic people. The former athlete is much more apt to become stiff in the joints than the classmate who cheered from the side-lines.

When we examine these once-energetic, now immobilized arthritics, we notice that their energies were directed along rather peculiar lines. The energy seemed to be compulsive, as if the person were driven to expend his forces. Where there is no compulsion for activity, the arthritic drives himself—and seldom for his own benefits.

We see among the arthritis patients the perfect housekeeper, the charitable worker, the club-woman, the philanthropist. They work hard at doing things for everyone except themselves. It almost seems as if they had a fear of doing what they want to do, getting what they want to have.

Let's consider again the animal who typifies fear-behavior —the lowly opossum. When he runs into a situation in which there is any threat, he plays dead; he becomes stiff and cold and remains that way until the danger has passed. It seems as if the arthritic patient were "playing possum"; perhaps he becomes cold and stiff in an attempt to escape from some imaginary danger, a danger which exists only within his own mental pattern. This sort of danger doesn't pass, of course, so he becomes progressively more stiff—as still as possible without dying completely. The imaginary danger can pass, naturally; dangers like that disappear promptly and completely when the person becomes aware of their falsity.

And here's another aspect to arthritis—the idea that the personality of the arthritic is as rigid and inflexible as his joints. We often see a tendency toward an uncompromising attitude, where everyone else must conform to the arthritic's beliefs and wishes. There's an attitude of "This is the way I say it is, and it's got to be that way." Frequently this is disguised by a false front of apparent compliance, with

166

the theme of, "Don't pay any attention to me—just go on and have a good time. I'll just sit here." And underneath the facade of sweetness is a core of sullen resentment and, as one writer puts it, "a whim of iron."

We can illustrate this by discussing the case of Dave. At the time he was first seen he was in his early forties, a dynamic and energetic man in spite of having a "poker spine." He was active in business and in community affairs and was the sort of man one called on when there was a Community Chest drive or a campaign to raise money for the hospital. It was noticeable that he was the boss of any committee to which he was appointed, whether he was the chairman or not. He had his ideas of how things should be done, and managed to get his own way by virtue of sheer stubbornness. If anyone tried to persuade Dave to change an opinion or alter a prejudice, he ran into a figurative wall as hard as the bones of Dave's back.

Dave also had an odd sense of possessiveness: he acted as if he got pleasure in owning, rather than using, and he sought to increase his possessions. Once he owned something he would not give it up, even if he had no further use for it; in this he imitated the attitude of the proverbial dog in the manger.

It was also noticeable that Dave had very few friends with whom he was on an even level of give-and-take. His companions were all the sort of people who were willing to obey him, to defer to him, to flatter and praise him—in short, people who did not try to change him.

To sum up, we could say that Dave was a combination of

conservatism, proprietorship and self-sacrifice. What better way could he act out this combination than by having—and keeping—arthritis?

The treatment he received followed the lines expressed previously: first, an increased knowledge of his own sensations, next an awareness of how he could create the pattern of sensations which went along with his arthritis. Did his back feel stiff? How could he make his back feel stiff? Could he make it feel even stiffer? How?

The "why" of his illness was also considered. In what situations had his back been stiff? Several interesting bits of information came out while pursuing this aspect. He recalled (and his mother corroborated this) that whenever he was frustrated as a child, his usual dramatization was to stiffen out and refuse to be moved until he got his own way. He was, moreover, a very fearful child, frequently worried about what might happen—and as he became fearful he would become tense with the emotions of his expectations.

Dave is still under treatment, so we cannot yet say what the final outcome of his case will be. It is noticeable, however, that he is having much less disability, that his back is beginning to become more flexible and much less painful.

OTHER DISEASES

Arthritis is not the only condition which affects the mobility of the joints. There is another condition in which the muscles or the tendons (which connect the muscles to the bones) are involved. The common term for this condition is "muscular rheumatism"; the medical profession usually calls it chronic fibrositis.

It is seen as a result of severe muscular strain or after a long period of disuse; use of the affected muscle is painful, so the muscle isn't used—which makes it more painful and less usable.

There is still another condition which imitates arthritis in its effects but is entirely different in its location. It is called "bursitis" and is an inflammation of a bursa, which is a little sac which acts as a pad between a joint and the muscle which run over it. If you feel the bony point of your shoulder, then touch the muscle about a finger's-breadth below that, you will be feeling the subacromial bursa, which is the one most often inflamed.

Shoulder bursitis is quite a painful and disabling condition; people who have this are not able to raise their arm more than a few inches from their side.

In all of these conditions we see a psychosomatic aspect to the complaint. In general, the people who suffer from such immobilizing disabilities are quite anxious. In anxiety, as we mentioned before, there is a considerable amount of muscular tension, as if the person wanted to make a movement and not make it at the same time.

This was seen in the case of John, who had a "paralyzed" arm. "Paralyzed" was the word he used to describe it—but it was not too accurate a word. About two years before he consulted a psychosomaticist, he had noticed that his right arm was occasionally painful and was becoming progressively weaker and less usable. With each passing month there would be a decrease in the motion of the elbow joint, so that he could neither bend his arm fully nor straighten it out. When he wanted to put his right hand in his pocket, he would grasp it with his left hand—as if it were some other person's hand—and shove it in. He could still write, but only with the greatest difficulty.

Examinations by neurologists and bone-and-joint specialists had disclosed no reason for John's trouble; they all agreed that there was nothing wrong with the arm except that it didn't work properly. As John said, "I knew that all along."

His general appearance gave the clue to the reasons for his disability: he was the picture of anxiety. He breathed shallowly, sighed frequently and sat on the edge of his chair as if ready to jump up and run at the slightest provocation. When he relaxed slightly from this tension, he appeared to slump into the apathetic attitude which says, in the language of body-movement, "Oh, what's the use—I give up."

Psychotherapy helped John (and note that it was John, not the doctor) to make this explanation: his attitude towards his father was one of great respect and admiration and, at the same time, extremely fearful. His father had been a harsh disciplinarian and had struck John frequently; and yet, in other respects he had been quite kind and considerate.

John recalled a scene when he was a young man in which he was ready to strike his father, and then found that he was afraid to do so. It was suggested that he try to complete this action which he had never finished, and pretend that he was punching his father in the face. He made the punching motion several times with increasing vehemence and with increasing strength, then broke into tears. When his weeping had finally subsided, he found that he could move his arm freely and easily.

There is, we feel, no simple explanation for this rapid recovery of the use of a "paralyzed" arm. One possibility is that John's anxiety had to do with his inability to make the choice of hitting his father or not hitting his father. He wanted to do both of them simultaneously—which is impossible—and compromised by doing neither, with this pseudo-paralysis as a result. When he learned in imagination that he could strike a blow, and when he acted out this fight which had never happened, he discovered that he could punch if he wanted to. With this discovery there was no longer a need for paralysis.

Remember, that is only one possible explanation; there may be others. We might note, however, that the action which John found himself able to take was sufficient to help him decide to cease paralyzing his own arm.

We suspect that a good many of the musculo-skeletal diseases are, in a sense, a form of self-created paralysis. It also seems to be within the realm of probability that when the person recognizes that he has some responsibility in maintaining his disease—when he can say, and can think, and can feel that he doesn't have to be crippled—he may have a good chance of recovery.

With anxiety there is tension; we usually speak of it as "nervous tension," but the tension is in the muscles. When the muscles act, the tension disappears. In John's case, the use of his muscles, and the knowledge that he could use them, enabled him to break out of the vicious circle of tension and disuse.

Muscular paralysis, incidentally, is not the only sort of function-failure which results from anxiety. Another one is deafness, in which the person acts as if he preferred not hearing. You have all seen people with diminished hearing who flatly refuse to wear a hearing-aid—and their refusal leads us to suspect that they are afraid to hear.

Every person who is deaf, therefore, might well consider these questions: what would happen to you if you heard something? What is it you don't want to hear? Whose voice wouldn't you want to hear? What are the advantages of not hearing? The disadvantages?

One last note on psychosomatic diseases and their treatment: in our discussion we have mentioned only those cases in which there was a successful outcome. We have done this deliberately, as we feel that you can learn more from this sort of case.

This does not mean that psychotherapy is always successful. It is not. There is still a great deal to be learned about the functioning of the human mind-body; we don't know all there is to know, and as long as we don't, we shall have failures as well as successes.

However, there is much that we do know—and by using our present knowledge as effectively as we can, we improve our chances for gaining further understanding.

There has been another deliberate omission: we haven't

mentioned all the diseases which are partially or wholly "psychosomatic." To do so, we feel, would only increase the weight of the book and add nothing to the message we are trying to put across.

We are trying to tell you of another way in which you can figure out what makes human beings so human; we want to give you the chance to do some figuring out by yourself, without cramming the knowledge into you. We hope that, with the principles discussed here, you will be able to reach some conclusions of your own.

CHAPTER VII

THE LANGUAGE OF LIVING

THE IMPORTANCE OF COMMUNICATION · VARIOUS TYPES OF COMMUNICATION · MISUSES OF COMMUNICATION · HOW TO MAKE THE MOST OF COMMUNICATION

BY THE time you have read this far, you will have acquired a pretty good understanding of how and why people become sick. We have also tried to show you some of the methods which are used in the psychosomatic treatment of various illnesses.

It now becomes necessary to back-track a little, to talk about theories again; we do this in order to round out the picture of the human being and to show what a vital part is played by communication in our view of the human-as-a-whole.

THE IMPORTANCE OF COMMUNICATION

If we were to draw up a list of the attributes which distinguish Man from the lower animals, we would have to put communication high on the list. It is true that animals, including the insects, have various means of imparting information. The bees, for example, have a sort of dance which says, "I have found a food-supply at such-and-such a distance in this-and-that direction." The men who have worked with chimpanzees report that these fascinating animals have a definite language of grunts and squeaks, with definite responses to each sort of "word." And anybody who has hunted with a dog learns to recognize the "Ow, ow, ow" that means, "I'm on the trail of something."

Animals seem to be able to "talk," in a limited sense of the word. But it is only Man who has learned how to talk about talking, and talk about talking about talking, and so on to almost infinite degrees of abstraction. And it is this ability, the ability to communicate with words, which has permitted Man to become the dominant species on this planet and, at the same time, to indulge in the unrealistic sort of conduct called neurosis.

VARIOUS TYPES OF COMMUNICATION

We have spoken of Man's ability to talk and to communicate. At first glance, communication and talking seem to be two words that mean the same thing.

But talking is not the only means of communication. It

is a means which is peculiar to us humans—but that doesn't mean that we can't communicate in other ways besides. As far as we know, we have at our disposal every means of communication which the lower animals have; they tend to be overlooked, hidden beneath the flow of words which is so great a part of our living.

These other means of communication might be compared to languages—other languages which we can understand, even though we are less aware of this ability. We all understand the language of smelling—we know how we feel when we smell a flower, and we recognize that that feeling is different from the one when we smell garbage. And then there's the language of touch—the communication of tactile sensations. We know that there is a difference between having your face touched by a barber and by a loved one; we know that silk feels different from sackcloth. Everything with which we come in contact carries a message to us.

We know the language of words—and we also know the language of sounds which are not words. There is the song of birds, the roar of the ocean, the babble of a woodland brook, the wind in the trees, music—none of these are words, but they are all communications, a part of our everyday language.

We should not overlook the language of taste, whereby we differentiate between wine and water, between ice-cream and dill pickles; we even know that there is a taste which goes with love, with fear or with sorrow. There is yet another language, the one which deals with movement. Whenever we hit a golf-ball squarely on the nose, or when

176

we feel our arms moving through the water as we swim, there is a type of bodily communication going on.

There is each of these languages, and other ones as well. Language doesn't have to be spoken. When we stop to think of it, our words are only symbols for these real sensations. Our sensations are the language of living—and words are the language for talking about living. Words are only letters put together, sounds which we make with our mouths; words are black marks on white paper or air-borne vibration. We accept them as symbols, just as we accept money as a symbol for our labors—but the symbol is never the thing which it stands for.

To a blind man, a verbal description of a beautiful scene is meaningless; to a person who has never loved, a love-song is just another tune. Words are a medium of exchange—but they can never replace the real wealth of sensation.

In sensations we have many languages; of even greater variety are the combinations of sensations. They never exist separately, in fact—within the whole person they are all going on in a constant chorus.

There is one of our languages, a combination of many, which is poorly understood: the language of feelings It is this language which communicates the state of well-being, or the condition of being ill. We know, for instance, that we can feel happy or sad or loving or angry; in short, we know that we have emotions.

The language of emotions is one which comes in for considerable suspicion in our society. It is misunderstood and usually condemned. From an early age, many of us are taught not to "show our emotions," and we are shown by example that "being emotional" is not the way to act.

Because of this attitude toward emotion, we are going to discuss the subject at considerable length, and try to show that the language of emotions is a most vital part of our living, and that we can learn to use it better.

Let us first consider how emotions evolved, and observe the way in which a one-celled animal, such as the amoeba, survives.

It has a means of responding to changes in the watery environment in which it lives. If there are certain chemical changes, it will move toward the point of maximum intensity of that change; this chemical change means food. With other chemical changes, it will move away from the source; that chemical means danger.

We have within our bodies a system of communication which seems to work similarly. We have groups of cells whose function is to create changes in the internal environment, helping the body to obtain what it wants or to flee from or reject what it doesn't want. The functioning of these cells can produce numerous and profound changes in the self-contained watery environment which is inside our skins; the temperature of the environment can be altered by the functioning of a group of cells called the thyroid gland; the sweetness (that is, the sugar content) is altered by the functioning of the cells of the pancreas and the adrenal glands; the hardness of the supporting structures of the body can be controlled by the cells of the parathyroid glands which control calcium metabolism.

You undoubtedly will recognize from this description that we are speaking of the endocrine system, which is made up of several different glands whose function seems to be the manufacture of chemical messengers. In response to certain stimuli, the glands will step up production of these chemical substances called hormones, and will pour the hormones into the blood-stream, whereby they are carried to all parts of the body.

This is a form of communication—but a rather nonspecific one. The messages which are transmitted are not addressed to any specific part of the body, but rather to the parts of the body which are capable of receiving the messages. Norbert Wiener, the author of *Cybernetics*, refers to these as messages addressed "To Whom It May Concern." To make another analogy, these messages carried by the hormones are like radio broadcasts.

There are many, many different aspects of endocrine function which can be discussed; for the purposes of this book, however, let us consider endocrine function only insofar as it relates to emotion.

Let us set up a rather specific definition of emotion, with the understanding that emotion includes what we are talking about—and a lot of other things·besides, which we don't mention. To define emotion, then, let us say that it is a feeling state, due to changes in the blood levels of various hormones, and with the apparent purpose of potentiating certain bodily responses.

Let us consider the third part of this definition, that emotions enable us to respond with greater intensity and greater effectiveness. Notice what happens when you try to open a door which ordinarily opens freely and find that the door sticks. You use the same amount of energy usually required to open the door, the door still sticks—so, you "get mad" at it. This process of "getting mad" usually includes frowning, increasing the tension in the jaw muscles and an almost indescribable complex of sensations which we recognize as the awareness of greater muscular strength.

You tried to open the door once; it stuck, so now you have greater energy at your command with which to jerk the door open in spite of its sticking.

We come now to the second part of the definition of emotion—the part which hormones play. In this marshalling of energy the effects seem to be due to a sudden outpouring from the adrenal gland of a substance called epinephrine. This results in an increased heart rate, a dilatation of the smaller bronchial tubes, an increase in the sugar content of the blood, an increase in the blood flow through the muscles, and so on.

In other words, there is a change in the general body state, which permits the utilization of greater force. Moreover, we are aware of these changes and can recognize them and label them, because they are communicated to us.

And this finally brings us to the first part of the definition —that emotion is a feeling-state. We recognize the occurrence of emotion because with it there is a pattern of sensations. It is a pattern made up of numerous elements, each of which has some special significance to the person feeling it. There are enough elements which are common to everyone so that we can have some degree of understanding; when another person says, "I am angry," you can, from your own experience with anger, infer many of the feelings which he is having. But my anger is *not* the same as your anger, or any other person's anger; there are differences as well as similarities.

In general, a person says that he is angry when he feels some or all of the following: tension of the jaw muscles, tension of the muscles of the forehead and around the eyes, which produces the grimace called "frowning" or "scowling," opening the mouth so as to bare the teeth, a tendency for the hands to assume the position of fists or claws, an increase in the heart rate, an increase in the respiratory rate, and a tendency for the body-as-a-whole to move towards the anger-causing object.

All these activities, with the sensations which lead us to the awareness of them, suggest that we are mobilizing the parts of the body for the purpose of overcoming an obstacle.

It should be emphasized again that an emotion is a *pattern* of activities and sensations. It seems to be the numerous elements which are common to several different emotional states which lead to confusion. As an example, in anger there is an increased rate of breathing; in sexual activities there is a similar increase. This does *not* mean that sex is the same thing as anger, although some people act as if it were. It would be equally false to say that a chair and a horse both have four legs and therefore should be responded to in the same fashion.

One more point in regard to emotion: when the energies of the body are mobilized by an emotional state, it seems as if these energies must be dissipated, must be released or expressed, must be utilized in some form. Each emotion seems to have its characteristic release-mechanism; we can release anger by aggressive activities, such as biting or pounding or kicking or clawing. We can release fear by running away or by shivering or by laughing or by becoming angry and then releasing the anger. We release the emotion called "disgust" by pushing, by vomiting, by defecating or by crying. We can release the fear of the expectation of our own death in crying. We can release the emotion called "sex" or "love" or "liking"—and all of these seem to be degrees of the same activity—by increasing the degree of contact with the object of affection.

It seems to be axiomatic that, when an emotion is once aroused, it *must* be expressed by some activity. If the appropriate activity is not available, the emotional force will trickle out by some other route. If you become angry and you do not express your anger in direct contact in fighting, or in chopping wood or punching a punching-bag, the anger will be released over a long, slow and usually painful period by such routes as headache, sinusitis, asthma, diarrhea and so on. If you become amorous and are not permitted to express your desire for contact in love-making, you may be forced to express it in the contact of destruction—in hitting, in making biting remarks, or in crushing into the state of acquiescence.

There is another aspect to this business of expressing

anger: you don't necessarily have to take it out on the object of your anger. You can express it toward some inanimate object, meanwhile pretending that it is the person who aroused your ire.

People do this sort of thing all the time, without recognizing what they're doing. For example, you get angry at your boss—but you don't say anything to him. Instead, you wait until you get home and bark at your wife, or scold your children. With this sort of displacement, however, you're apt to get other feelings, such as shame at your unfairness If you direct your expression of anger at a pillow it may be as effective, and much less disturbing to your family. The important thing is to keep fully in awareness the real object of your rage.

In this discussion of the language of emotion, you may have noted that we discussed it coldly and factually—but although emotions are a fact, they're *not* cold. We can use words to talk about emotions—but the words are not the feeling. Emotions can be warm—we can have the warmth of friendship, the heat of anger, the burning of passion. We can talk about them coolly, but that does not lower their temperature.

In spite of any atempts at scientific exactitude, emotions can never be completely understood as words. They exist as feelings, and the words we use to talk about them will always be pale shadows compared to the reality.

And while we are discussing the "unspeakability" of emotion, we might also mention another phase of feelings which is frequently overlooked: the contagion of feelings. Have you ever noticed how a happy person can enter a room and everything begins to brighten up? Have you ever seen how the fun of a party can be dampened by the presence of one fearful person? Have you ever met somebody and knew immediately that you were going to like him?

It doesn't seem to be what these people say or do, or how they look; their presence alone is enough to carry a message. Call it telepathy, call it an "aura," call it what you will—it is still a real factor in human relationships. We can recognize it and we can acquire it—but first we need to learn about our own feelings.

But let's go back to something a little more concrete—the other form of communication which goes on within the body. We refer, of course, to the nervous system and its function as an internal language.

The nervous system is a complicated set-up which gives us specific information. By means of its function we get specific data from, and issue specific commands to, certain specific parts of the body. You feel a fly on your nose; the nervous system carries the message, "There is an irritant here and now"; the information is integrated in the brain; the appropriate muscles are energized to produce the sort of motion best calculated to remove the irritant.

When this integration process of choosing an appropriate response goes astray, we are apt to see those bizarre activities which we call psychosis or neurosis or psychosomatic illness. Suppose that you try to get rid of the fly on the end of your nose by cutting your nose off, or by hitting yourself on the nose with a piece of lead pipe, or by setting fire to the house—your conduct would be referred to as eccentric, to say the least.

But note that you would be responding to a specific stimulus in ways which are effective; the trouble with them is that they are *too* effective, much more effective than they need to be. And why did you do it? Because of certain past experiences in which you learned that the stimulus of fly-on-nose is terribly dangerous, requiring heroic methods of response.

This discussion is to emphasize one point: any conduct, no matter how bizarre or insane, has a purpose and is based on some experiences in which it was learned, however mistakenly, that it was necessary. When we view the problem of functional disorders in this way, we can find a solution much more often than if we dismiss it as, "Well, that's just the way some people act."

To express this another way, "insane" conduct in any degree is not unreasonable when considered in the light of the person's experience; what is unreasonable, however, is that the person acts as if this were the *only* way in which he could respond. The scale which runs from sanity to insanity, or from health to illness, is made up of choices; each additional choice which becomes available brings the person closer to health.

We can speak of "insane" or "eccentric" conduct, then, as a sort of mis-function of communication. The message, "Here is a minor irritation," has been garbled to read, "Here is a threat to your life." The message is correctly communicated—but something has gone wrong with the interpretation.

You may have noticed that we have said nothing about memory. There are numerous reasons for this, one being that memory-function is such a complicated and poorly understood subject. The medical profession is still in disagreement about what a person can remember, under what circumstances he is capable of remembering, and for how long he can remember.

Recent investigations, however, have shown that there seem to be two levels of memory—one, where sensations are felt and then recorded, the second, where these sensations are grouped into patterns, so that a reaction can be made.

To give an example, one investigator worked with a series of patients who were unconscious as a result of head injury. While they were unconscious he touched them in various ways, said several things to them. After they had recovered consciousness, he asked them if they could recall anything that was said or done to them during the unconscious period; as might be expected, the answer was, "No—nothing." Then he hypnotized these people—and during the state of hypnosis, they were able to recall at least parts of the words and actions.

This is, we feel, an important experiment; it brings up many questions which might be asked. Is a person storing "memories" of his sensations, even while he is unconscious? What is consciousness, and how does it differ from unconsciousness? At what age does this "memory" storage begin? At what age can we begin to recall these stored facts?

186

We don't propose to answer these questions in this book. They are asked in order to show you that such questions can be asked, that we still don't have all the answers, that perhaps some of the answers we have today will be shown to be incorrect tomorrow.

In discussing memory as a part of communication, however, we can mention this: you can listen to the language of your memories in several ways. You can listen to it as if Memory were a dictator, who says, "You did it this way in the past; you must do it this way now." Or you can listen to Memory as if it were an adviser, who says, "Here is one way in which it was done in the past; don't you want to do it better this time?"

So let's say that "memories" of sensations, of patterns of sensations and of our reactions to these sensations are stored somewhere and somehow. There is communication with memories, too; we can send messages to be "remembered" and we can get messages out of storage again. We can also —and this is important in psychosomatic illness—make use of memories which we don't know that we have. It is in these memories that the "why" of illness usually lies, as you have seen from the discussion of cases.

So far, we have talked mostly about the communication that goes on within a person—the messages from the various sense-organs, the messages to the various effect-organs, such as the muscles.

Now let us discuss the communication that goes on between a person and the rest of the world, especially the world of other people.

187

If you were to ask one of your friends how he communicates, the answer would probably be, "By speaking and by writing, of course." That's true—but it's certainly not the whole truth. It's probably less than a third of the truth.

It might be more accurate to say that we communicate by means of our actions. We act with our vocal cords—but we also act with the muscles of our faces, with our glands, with our whole bodies. And communication does not occur unless there is interaction between the one putting out the information and the one receiving it; it's a two-way process.

We act—and we also communicate—on three different levels: the verbal, the emotional and the actional. You can communicate your feelings toward someone you love by using the words, "I love you." You can also tell her this by your feelings toward her—your warmth, your willingness to give and receive contact with her. You can also tell her that you love her with your actions—by doing the things she likes done.

As you can see, these three levels overlap considerably, and are not actually separate. We make the separation only verbally, and we do so in order to show you that there are other means of communication besides words. We also point out that there are these three levels because some people act as if there were no connection between them.

Whenever a person says one thing and does something different, it indicates that there is a conflict going on within him. He is acting as if he were two people—one who does the saying, another who does the doing—and neither one is in communication with the other.

Communication—it's a complex subject. Man has accomplished a great deal with communication—but he has barely scratched the surface. Our civilization has developed the telegraph, the telephone, radio, television—but what are we doing about our own intrapersonal communications? We can bounce a radar beam off the moon—but Man may find himself out in Space, all alone, if he neglects listening to the language of living.

We can rediscover the language of living; we can become adept at it. And out of the language of living, we can find our greater potentialities.

MISUSES OF COMMUNICATION

Communication, as we said, is the means of acquiring or imparting information. When we get information, we expect that it will be accurate, that we can depend upon it, that we won't be hurt when we use it. We expect our information to be consistent, unambiguous; if it isn't clear and concise, we become confused.

We also seem to expect that the information communicated to us on the various levels should be consistent. But is it?

Take the case of Bobbie, a four-year-old boy. He asks his mother if he can go out and play. Mother is a little out of sorts that day, so she snaps, "No—you stay in the house."

"But why can't I?"

"I don't want you to. Now you be quiet—I'm not going to argue with you."

Bobbie puckers up his face and starts to cry.

"Stop that crying!" his exasperated mother yells. "You can't go out and that's all there is to it!"

Bobbie wails louder—and his mother slaps him. "There—that'll teach you not to cry. Now sit down and behave yourself."

Bobbie sits down, confused and bewildered. He's angry, fearful, sad and defiant, all at the same time. He scowls and thinks about what he's going to do when he grows up. He is tense, and he squirms around in the chair in an involuntary release of the pressure of his emotional energy.

His mother feels a little ashamed at losing her temper, yet tries to convince herself that her actions were justified. She sees her son's restlessness increasing and finally she relents.

"You can go out now, dear—but there's something I want to tell you first. You know that Mother loves you—but she doesn't want you to be a cry-baby. And you have to learn to do what I tell you—Mother knows what's best for you."

This sounds like a rather common household tragedy, doesn't it? Let's look at it from the standpoint of communication, however, and see what Bobbie might have learned from the experience.

First, how consistent was the information which he got? He saw that Mother's face was flushed and heard her yell at him; previous experience told him that that meant she was angry. She also acted angry, in that she slapped him. That information is pretty consistent. But then he has to reconcile this with the words, "Mother loves you," "Mother

THE LANGUAGE OF LIVING

doesn't want you to be a cry-baby," "Mother knows what's best," and so on. And first wanting to go out was dangerous; then suddenly it became safe.

If Bobbie were to take literally what his mother has said —and we know that children are quite literal-minded—he might learn from this experience that being loved is also being slapped: that asking questions leads to punishments; that punishment is "the best thing." It's quite confusing— and the confusion could have been avoided if Mother had made her words consistent with her deeds.

An even more insidious form of the misuse of communication is seen when a person mislabels his own feelings. The doctor sees this so often—the patient says, "I feel just terrible—I ache all over, and I'd give anything to feel better," and the patient's actions during this little speech indicate that he's proud of being ill, that this illness is valuable and that he's going to hold on to it.

Or another example is the person who seems to enjoy martyrdom, who gasps, moans, then sighs, "I'm all right— don't pay any attention to me."

Are these people "faking"? Does this sort of behavior mean that the illness is unreal? No, definitely not. It indicates, rather, that they haven't learned how to say with words the things they are feeling in their bodies. The meanings of their communications are confused: they say things with one meaning, they do things with another meaning. This very confusion leads to a change in the way they feel —but they don't feel as they say they are feeling. Doesn't this sound confusing? It's this kind of confusion which leads to the mistakes in the learning pattern we were talking about a while back, mistakes which never got the chance to be corrected.

We have observed that people seem to feel a lot better when they get their communications untangled. Not only do they understand themselves better, but they are more understandable to others—and thus they can come into closer contact with other people.

HOW TO MAKE THE MOST OF COMMUNICATION

You can, if you like, make some experiments which will help you to understand this process of communication better. Some of these experiments will be discussed in the last chapter—but let us indicate the purpose of them now.

One can learn more about these messages which come from the various parts of the body—and, after doing so, can take the sort of actions which are appropriate to the message received. For example, you can become more aware of such sensations as sights, sounds, tastes and touch feelings. As you do so, you will find that your experiences will be much more meaningful to you. You will be able to find something new in each experience. There will be less likelihood of your saying, "Oh, it's the same old thing, day after day. I'm so bored with this monotonous job I have."

When you come right down to it, no two events are ever completely alike and nothing is ever the same. Each moment of living brings a new pattern of sensations—and if you are aware of your sensations, you can recognize that it is new. If you ignore your sensations, you tend to miss out on so many of the good things of life—the little simple pleasures which make the difference between happiness and boredom.

Of course, not all our sensations are pleasurable. There are such things as plain, sorrow or disappointment. You can become aware of these feelings, too—and when you do, you can do something about it. If you feel sad, and you brush off the feelings of sorrow, saying, "I'm just going to try to forget about this," the sorrow will persist. If you will become aware of your sorrow, and then *feel* sorry, *act* sorry, *be* sorry—there is a better chance that the sorrow will vanish. The business of being sorry is completed and done with, instead of being a nagging factor which enters into every experience.

You might also consider that you, as an organism, have certain needs, and that you can know about these needs by being aware of your internal communications. An example of this is often seen in the medical condition known as "pica," or perverted appetite. There is the practice, common among pregnant women, of picking plaster off the wall and eating it. The medical profession found this horrible, at first—until the doctors recognized that there is an increased demand for calcium during pregnancy, and that this was one way of supplying the demand. The lower animals behave similarly: a cow that doesn't get enough salt in her food may get it by eating the clothes off the line, or the dog, ordinarily a meat-eater, will eat quantities of grass under certain conditions of illness.

In other words, we can be aware of our needs—and we

have that awareness only so long as we don't ignore our own sensations.

We can also improve our communications with other people; we can do this by being more aware. You have no doubt observed that when you meet someone, you can pretty well tell how he feels. If he is confident, secure and happy, you can tell that easily by the way he speaks and acts; if he is timid and afraid, you can recognize that. You can go a step further, as your awareness improves, and recognize that these feelings are *his*, not yours, and that you can be influenced by them or not, as you prefer.

Suppose you meet someone who is frightened and defensive, so defensive that he has to attack everyone who comes near him. You can sense his fear—and, if you're like most people, you can react by becoming fearful too, without knowing why. But you can do something else—by being aware of his fearfulness, and recognizing it, you can then take whatever action seems best to alleviate his fear. When you can do this, you will find that you're not the slightest bit fearful—the chances are that you won't even think about being afraid of this stranger. He, in feeling your lack of fear, will become less fearful too.

Finally, you can improve your abilities in communication by saying what you mean. It isn't always possible to do this, of course; our social conventions frequently demand the use of the "little white lie." But we suggest that you try to make your words consistent with your feelings as often as you can. If you feel unhappy, try saying that you are, instead of "Everything is fine." If you like your wife's cook-

ing, or your friend's new car, or your secretary's hair-do—
tell them how you feel, how much you like it, instead of
condemning with the faint praise of, "Pretty good," or "It's
all right, I guess."

You might also try to be more outspoken about your dis-
likes as well. If your wife has some annoying mannerisms,
you might discuss them with her, rather than bottling up
the feeling of annoyance. Remember, however, that you
have to be ready to hear about some of the annoying things
which you do—communication works best when it is a two-
way set-up.

We think that you'll find it a fascinating experiment to
open up the channels of communication within yourself,
and between yourself and the people and things around
you. Like every experiment, it may not be too easy at first.
You may find it disturbing or you may feel that you aren't
getting any place. There may be times when you feel like
saying, "Oh, to hell with it!" and sliding back into the old
ways of less-than-complete living. That's to be expected.

But keep on trying—at your own rate, according to your
needs and desires. Gradually you will become more fluent
in expressing the language of living, more understanding of
the joy it contains.

CHAPTER VIII

HOW TO USE WHAT YOU LEARN

EXERCISES IN SELF-AWARENESS · HOW TO OVERCOME PAIN
(WITHOUT DRUGS) · HOW TO BE HAPPIER

AFTER having read this far, you can see that you can apply some of these principles to yourself. You will certainly recognize that you have some fixed reaction patterns, and you might even recall how you learned them. Maybe you are training your children to react in the same way, even though you say that such behavior is silly or "bad." And maybe you'd like to do something about it.

Of course this brings up the question: is it a good idea for a person to dabble with his own thinking processes? Isn't this infringing on the province of the doctor? Isn't there some possibility of something going wrong?

If you have any doubts about the wisdom of performing any of these exercises, it is better for you not to try them. If you wonder whether or not it is advisable, we suggest

196

that you consult with your medical adviser and get his opinion. It is probable, we suspect, that your doctor will give you the "go-ahead" signal, as he will recognize that the principles expressed in this book are in no wise contradictory to medical literature. It's a good idea to check with him, nonetheless.

EXERCISES IN SELF-AWARENESS

It has been pointed out earlier in this book that people tend to act, during moments of stress, in rather rigid patterns. A man will see blood and he will faint—every time. Another person may be required to talk to a business superior and he will get a pain in his stomach—again every time.

We can say that this sort of reaction results in a confusion between what is going on Here and Now and what went on at some previous time. There *was* a time when a person saw blood and he felt faint—but at that time he saw some definite sights, smelled some specific smells, heard some specific noises and words, felt some definite sensations. There is a similarity between what happened There and Then and what is happening Here and Now—and that is the sight of blood. There are also numerous differences—different circumstances, different environments, different ages, different sensations.

But the person is acting as if he were not aware of the differences: instead he is responding as if one single sensation, the sight of blood, made the two entirely different situations into a single one. And so he faints again. This

197

knowledge is not in the level of mental activity where he can remember all about it and can talk about it, but it's there just the same.

It has been found that a person can decrease the probability of making an "every time" reaction by becoming aware of his present-time sensations. By so doing, it seems that he acquires more information for differentiating between the old experience and the current one—and when he can do so, he is then able to choose between fainting and not fainting. After all, if you can't see any difference between two chairs, it doesn't matter which one you take. If there is a difference between them, then there is something which makes a choice possible.

How do we increase this awareness of present time? It's very simple—and at the same time, quite difficult.

First, let us say that it's similar to concentration. You know that when you're doing something that is very, very interesting, you tend to focus your attention on that and on nothing else. Perhaps you're reading and the radio is turned on. If the book is what you call "a good one," it is probable that you don't know whether the music issuing from the radio is Bach, boogie or be-bop. In other words, the focus of your attention (or awareness) is directed *at* the book, *away from* the radio.

Compare that with the mythical man who faints every time he sees blood. In that situation his attention is focussed entirely on the blood, away from everything else. And we suggest that if he changes his focus of attention, there will be much less chance for him to crumple up and fall over.

It's obvious that this is not startlingly new. We all seem to know instinctively that distraction of attention is an effective way of changing a person's behavior. What is new to most people, however, is that one can do this as a practical technique according to certain specific principles and with predictable results. Furthermore, by practicing during moments when there is a minimum of stress, you will have learned means of coping with an emergency when it arises.

So here is the first exercise: select some time and place where there is as little confusion as possible and where you can be reasonably certain that you won't be interrupted. Lying down on your bed in a darkened room with the door closed is a good example.

All right—you're lying down, everything is peaceful and quiet. Then you start to notice all the sensations which you can feel Here and Now. You might try to verbalize subvocally—that is, talk to yourself so softly that no one but you could hear it—and make a list of what you notice. And it's a good idea to use the words "Here" and "Now" in every sentence, so as to keep your attention focussed on what actually is Here and Now.

It might sound something like this: "Here and Now I can feel the pressure on my back and the backs of my legs as I lie on the bed. My legs are crossed, Here and Now, and my left ankle is lying on my right one. Here and Now my arms are at my sides, and I can feel the texture of the sheets with my fingers. Here and Now I can hear the sound of the steam in the radiator pipes."

While you are doing this you will probably become aware of some sensations which are not due to present-time stimuli. You might develop an itch on your face. Is there something tickling your face, like a feather or a fold of blanket? If not, just notice that you can have a response which is *not* due to an adequate present-time stimulus, and go back to the recapitulation of what is actually Here and Now.

Notice how long you can keep up this procedure before being distracted by inappropriate sensations, before straying from the exercise of awareness of the Present. Most people report that they can do this consistently for only a minute or so, that if they try to keep it up any longer, their thoughts wander off or they become very nervous or they fall asleep. If that's what happens to you, you don't have to be discouraged; instead, you can recognize that here is a sort of exercise which is challenging and which is much more interesting than it would be if it were as easy as falling off a log. You will find that with each time you try the experiment, your awareness of Here and Now will increase.

That's the first exercise—simply learning how to focus your attention on all the sensations, one by one, which you are experiencing at a particular moment and as a result of that moment's stimuli.

The second exercise—and it seems to be best to try at least ten or twelve sessions of the first exercise before going on to the second—deals with the sensations which are *not* due to present time stimuli. Let's suppose that you have noticed a stiffness in the muscles at the back of your neck.

Is there any stimulus for that tension? Is it a result of the position in which your head is lying? Is the pillow pressing into your neck?

Notice at this point that you're looking for stimuli, and not reasons which are rational or rationalizing. Try not to dismiss the sensation by saying, "Oh, that's just the pain I always have," or, "I guess I'm just tired and nervous and I can't relax!" After all, such rationalizing is probably what you have been doing all along—and you might notice that it hasn't enabled you to overcome the pain in your neck. Instead, simply note that you have such a sensation and then proceed to the second step of manipulating it. Try to increase the tension in the particular group of muscles around the neck—then relax. Increase the tension again—then relax. Try to set up a rhythmic exercise of tension and relaxation and notice what happens.

Maybe the tension will disappear entirely or almost entirely; then again, maybe it won't. If it doesn't, try to let this neck-muscle tension spread to other parts of your body. Try to do with the muscles of your forearms what you are doing with the muscles of your neck—and keep up that rhythm for a while. Then let the muscles of the legs, the shoulders, the chest, the abdomen, the hips and the face also take part in this exercise. In other words, try to convert this localized tension into a whole-body tension—and continue to increase it and decrease it rhythmically.

Sooner or later the muscles will feel fatigued and you will probably notice that it becomes more and more difficult to create the tension, and more and more easy to let the muscles relax. When you get to that point, stop; that's the end of the session.

After you have familiarized yourself with the second step, and can manipulate muscle tensions with ease—and, we predict, with benefit to your general bodily state—you might notice that something else is putting in an appearance. You might observe that there are some emotional states which accompany these various sorts of muscle-tension—and that's the third step in self-awareness.

In this third step we ask you not only to manipulate, but to *express*. Let us suppose that you are practicing tightening the muscles of the back of your neck, and that the tension seems to be spreading to the muscles of your throat. You become aware that you feel as if you had a lump in your throat—just as if you were going to cry. When such is the case, try to let the tears come out. Don't try to force them out at first—simply keep on with your tension-relaxation exercises, trying neither to cry nor to hold back the tears.

It is probable that here you will run into a conflict, especially if you are a man. In our society, most males are trained to be impassive, not to show emotion and to feel ashamed if they do let any such "weakness" as tears become noticeable. The expression of anger is fairly acceptable, although there is considerable pressure put on all of us not to lose our tempers.

If you find that you have this conflict, please notice this: you can cry if you want to, but you don't have to cry. The mere awareness that you feel like crying is often sufficient to permit these chronic tensions to relax. But if, on the other hand, you do cry, you don't have to be ashamed of it. It appears that crying is *one—not* the only—method of releasing the energy of certain emotions. It can be released in other ways.

This brings us to another form of emotional tension and emotional expression—anger. Let us suppose that you are again working with tension in the neck muscles; you have let this tension spread to your arms and become aware that you are clenching your fists as if you were angry. If such is the case, try to let this anger come out in some form of activity, such as pounding the bed, or wrestling with the pillow. Recognize, if you please, that you are developing an unusual sort of energy which enables you to make an unusual sort of response—and make it, if you want to.

Perhaps you won't want to. Maybe you'll think that it's silly for a grown man or an adult woman to lie on a bed and pound on it for no apparent reason whatsoever. That's right—it is silly. Anger is a force to be used for overcoming obstacles, and there's no obstacle here to overcome.

But let's take another look at it. Maybe there is an obstacle—your own wish not to express anger or any other emotion. That's the way the mind seems to work: we set up an obstacle for ourselves, then set up another obstacle which will prevent us from coming to grips with the first obstacle, and then another obstacle which will prevent us from coming in contact with the second barrier, and so on. The force which helps us to overcome these fences in the path of our living seems always to be the same—and we usually call it "anger."

Sooner or later, then, you will learn that, when you recognize the feeling of anger in yourself, it is wise to take some form of bodily activity. Pounding the bed or choking the pillow is one form: so is a long, brisk walk, or chopping wood, or punching a bag, or pounding a piano. True, you can also beat your wife or spank your children—but what about the reaction you would set up in them?

We are, of course, getting into a subject which is complicated and not too well-understood by the vast majority of people. When we deal with emotions, we are dealing with the whole system of driving forces and evaluations and wishes and desires that are peculiar to us humans.

Emotions can't all be dealt with simply—but we can deal with them one at a time. In fact, it seems that working with emotions on a simple and primitive level, where one considers each sensation that goes to make up the total picture is a much better and more effectual way than to try to understand the whole thing at once.

We suggest, therefore, that at first you not try to figure out at whom or at what you're angry. Instead, try to increase the awareness of your anger, noticing the pattern of sensations which combine to make it a recognizable entity and learn that you don't have to bottle it up.

This also applies to the other emotions and emotional releases. In fear, for example, it is a big help to realize that you don't have to be afraid of being afraid. You can become fearful and notice the sensations which go with it; then you can let these sensations build up until they are ready to pour out in some sort of activity such as goose-flesh, trembling, chattering of teeth or curling up into a ball. The knowledge that you *can* do this, if you want to, seems to carry with it the realization that you don't have to if you don't want to.

In doing these exercises, however, it is advisable not to be content with the mere saying of the words, "I can become angry," or, "I can cry." Such a parroting of words is incomplete unless it is accompanied by the appropriate bodily activity.*

It is hoped that by this time you will recognize that these exercises are performed by performing them—not by just reading them.

In a sense, the description of these methods is a "How to" sort of thing, like "How to play golf" or "How to raise tropical fish" and playing golf requires activity, not just "book learning."

You will also recognize that you don't have to do these exercises any more than you have to run out and purchase a set of golf-clubs or an aquarium. It might even be that you will enjoy the lack of compulsion, the feeling that you don't have to do anything about what you have learned in your reading of this book. After all, there is so much compulsion in this society of ours—haven't you heard it in radio ad-

---

* These exercises—or, rather, experiments in self-awareness—are only the primary steps of a system which has been worked out by Frederick Perls, M.D. and his associates, Dr. Ralph Hefferline and Dr. Paul Goodman. If you are interested in pursuing this sort of self-investigation further, it is recommended that you read their book *Gestalt Therapy: Excitement and Growth in the Human Personality* (Julian Press, New York, 1951). Appreciation is also gratefully expressed to these authors for their permission to use this material.

vertising?—that an awareness of your ability to choose might be refreshing.

Maybe you're just not interested in self-awareness—if so, that's your choice. But there is one aspect of this work which is extremely helpful: the control of pain.

HOW TO OVERCOME PAIN WITHOUT DRUGS

It would be nice if this chapter could be started with a glib definition of pain. There just doesn't seem to be a good, all-inclusive definition, however. Pain is one of those words which everyone thinks he understands; it is so common a word that a person seldom thinks of the need for defining it. It might even be that it can't be defined; in a definition there is an attempt at agreement, and there is very little agreement about what constitutes pain. Moreover, pain is a uniquely personal experience, and it is obvious that one person cannot have another's sensations.

In order to have some idea of what we're talking about, let's say that we use the word "pain" in referring to a sensation or group of sensations which accompanies interference with functioning of part or all of the body. If we can say that pain has a purpose, we would say that it is a danger signal—a sensation which warns us that function is being hampered in some way. Pain is, therefore, a sign that action should be taken; it implies that if action is not taken, the survival chances of the organism are going to decrease.

Suppose that you have a toothache: that means that something has happened so that the tooth isn't functioning as well as it can, and that you'd better find out why so that

206

you can do something about it. Incidentally, the pain doesn't tell you what you should do; it merely suggests that something should be done.

At this point we can make a statement in regard to pain: once pain has served its purpose, it is no longer necessary to have it! There's a statement which is sure to arouse a good deal of argument. How can you prove that the statement is incorrect? How can we demonstrate that we have sufficient reasons for making the statement?

Here's an experiment which you can try on yourself or on another person: whenever you see an injury (and let's hope that it's trivial) of recent origin, have the person try to replay the pattern of sensation and to express it. Say that your wife has burned her arm while taking a hot dish out of the oven. You ask her to sit down and tell you all about it. (It seems to help if you will also ask her to close her eyes; opened eyes increase one's awareness of the present, and you, in a sense, are asking her to deal with things which *were* present.)

As she tells you about her painful experience, try to help her to relate the pain to all the other sensations which she had at that moment: what did she hear at the moment of being burned? Ask her to imagine that she is hearing those sounds again, and feeling the pain again. What was she looking at when the burn was received? Ask her to imagine again that she is looking at the oven door, the hot dish, the pot-holder in her hand—and to feel again the pain of the burn. Ask her about the sights, the sounds, the odors, the tastes, the bodily positions and movements, including what she said—and have her relate each one of these sensations to the sensation of being burned.

Another sensation which she might consider is her emotional response: was she frightened? Angry? Was she glad?

Perhaps it might sound strange to suggest that a person might feel glad about being injured, but it's a possibility which might be overlooked. If a person predicts that he is going to be injured, and then is injured, there is a certain satisfaction at having the prediction "come true." It is as if the person were to say, "I said I was going to hurt myself, and I did hurt myself, and now I'm glad."

This process of relating the various sensations other than the burn to the sensation of the burn is repeated at least six to ten times, or until no further associations can be made. To put it another way, you are trying to help your wife recall *all* the sensation of that moment in time, including the pain, and to help her recognize that these sensations are not in themselves painful.

In the vast majority of the cases, the pain of the injury disappears almost completely and is not likely to return. It also seems that injuries treated in this way heal faster and with fewer complications than if given only the more conventional treatment of ointments, pain-relievers, etc.

A good example of this technique is given in *New Ways in Discipline* by Dr. Dorothy W. Baruch (Whittlesey House, New York, 1949); she tells the story of the little boy who was injured. His mother, instead of making the usual remarks such as, "Don't cry," "Don't be a sissy," said "Let's sit down and you tell me all about it." After he had told his mother all about it, the boy said, "Now it doesn't hurt any more."

A few cases have been seen where the person reports that this doesn't work. When such is the case, one can usually find that the person has not considered all the possible sensations, or that there was some emotion which required expression.

Perhaps it would not be amiss at this point to describe something which came under my personal observation. My eleven-year-old daughter was playing with a stick of punk last Fourth of July and dropped the burning ember on her forearm. She has been taught how to direct her attention to injuries, as previously described, so she attempted to do so. She said that it wouldn't stop hurting, and it could easily be seen that she was acting annoyed about it.

"I've done everything you told me to do, and it still won't go away!" she said, and her voice tones were definitely those of resentment directed at everyone and at the pain itself.

I suggested that she try to think of a reason for burning herself—any reason, no matter how silly. "Well, I might burn myself if I was mad at myself," she replied.

I asked her then to act as if she was *really* mad at herself —what could she do? She replied that she might hit herself, and I asked her to do this a few times. She did so, then said, "That's silly."

I then asked her to get mad at something outside herself; she happened to be sitting on the floor at that time, so she chose to "get mad" at the floor, which she did by pounding on it with her hands. A couple of blows, then she laughed. When I asked her how the pain was, she said, "It's all gone," and she walked out of the house singing merrily.

Please note that this procedure is recommended for use in *recent* injuries, those for which there is an obvious cause within the last hour or so. We advise caution in attempting to apply this to pains not of recent external origin, such as headaches, stomach-aches and the like. In such a case, the attempt to recall all the details of the original injury may take the patient into situations where it might take expert assistance to extricate him. If there is a pain *not* of recent origin, it is safer to use the "self-awareness" technique, as previously described. Of course, if any pain is unduly persistent, a medical opinion is in order.

In other words, when the injury has occurred recently, you can try to find out both how and why the pain began; when there is no obvious present-time reason for a pain, it is probably better to limit your attempts to finding out *how* the pain might be produced, leaving the "why" to someone well-trained in the methods.

The reason for this advice is that occasionally, when one attempts to recall experiences in the far past, there is a stirring up of severe pain. This can be dealt with easily by a competent therapist, but a discussion of the methods is beyond the scope of this book.

There has been a sort of response which is noteworthy in the people who have worked with this approach to pain: after a while, one seems to lose the fear of pain.

Any doctor or dentist or nurse, anyone whose work involves the inflicting of pain, is well aware that most people suffer more from their fear of pain than they do from the pain itself. Take the man who doesn't like to go to a dentist; he sits in the chair, rigid, ready to jump, flinching from the slightest touch. He has not had any pain—but his anticipation of the pain has caused more discomfort than the dentist could.

Here's another experiment which you might try: the next time you are faced with the prospect of being hurt, try to find out just what "hurt" means. Let's consider a session with the dentist, again—the dentist is already such a bugaboo to most people that he makes a good example. As you sit in his chair, waiting for him to start drilling, think about how you're going to feel the sensation of having your teeth worked on. When the drilling starts, focus on the sensations of the drill in your mouth: does it feel hot? Cold? What is the sound? Is there any sense of vibration? What position does your jaw take? Where are the dentist's hands? Can you feel the mirror as well as the drill? Notice what you're looking at. In other words, focus your attention on the sensations, rather than on your interpretation of the sensations, or your expectations of sensations.

You might consider this idea: *fear is based on anticipation.* When something is about to happen, and you know pretty well what that something is going to be, you tend to be rather calm about it. When you're in a situation when you don't know what the outcome is going to be, when you can't predict what's going to happen, then you tend to become fearful.

One more little technical device for decreasing the intensity of pain could be mentioned. It's an ancient one, known to every mother almost instinctively: distraction of attention. We observe that when a person is having discomfort, his attention is pretty well fixed on his pain. He'll talk about something for a while, then the conversation will veer back to how uncomfortable he is. He'll look at the flowers you brought him, then focus his attention on whatever is bothering him.

Anything which will draw his attention away from the pain will lessen the pain. Asking for advice on a weighty problem is one way; telling funny stories is another way; bringing the conversation around to some emotionally-charged topic is yet another way.

A nurse in a mid-western hospital was a master at using this last method. She was so good at it, in spite of the fact that she apparently wasn't aware of what she was doing, that every doctor wanted her when he had a really sick patient. The patients disliked her cordially; as they expressed it, "She makes me so damned mad—I'm going to get well in a hurry so I can get rid of her."

You may notice that no mention has been made in these discussions of the use of medications. We have spoken of infections, but haven't mentioned the antibiotics; we have spoken of pain, yet haven't discussed aspirin; we have mentioned "nervousness" without speaking of the use of sedatives. These omissions have been deliberate, and they do *not* mean that the use of medications is "bad." What we are trying to do in this book is simply to point out that

212

there are *other* methods which have also been proven useful. They are methods which depend upon a person's ability to direct his reactions, instead of giving him something new to react to.

HOW TO BE HAPPIER

By knowing how to manage your reactions, you are more self-sufficient, less a potential victim of any unwanted change in your environment.

And what do we mean by "managing one's reactions"? Let's take a look at the person who is chronically angry. Everything "makes him mad"—his wife, his boss, his children, the weather, the political situation. He says so, too—and notice how he says it: "It *makes* me mad."

He is speaking as if he had no choice; his children yell, and they make him—they *force* him—to experience a pattern of sensations he calls being "mad." But do they force him? *Must* he have that reaction and only that reaction? Isn't it possible that he might have a choice in this sort of situation?

We think so. But how can he go about reaching that state where he can choose to be angry or not angry?

The first step, we think, is to make a revision in one's ways of speaking about such reactions. Instead of the expression, "It makes me mad," consider this: "My children yell, and I become angry."

Do you notice the difference? The first statement indicates a reaction which one is forced to make; the second indicates that this is *his* reaction. And if it's his own re-

213

action, then he can change it, if he wants to. The reaction is, as we have pointed out before, a result of numerous experiences in the past when he learned that children's yelling was the signal for getting out the record marked "Anger" and starting to play it.

That's the first step—the awareness of a response-pattern to a stimulus. The next step is to try making a different response—any response, no matter how ridiculous, so long as it's different. Suppose that you are one of those people who "get mad" when the children yell; the next time they lift their little voices, act as if you were crying. Of course, that's not a sensible adult reaction—but try it on for size anyhow. Make a good act out of it, too; try to show yourself what a really fine "ham" you can be. Then notice what happened to your anger.

Are you more angry? Less angry? Just notice it so you can remember it and compare it with previous patterns of response.

Then the next time the children begin to scream merrily, pretend to be afraid. Let the act of fear be a total bodily response: shiver and shake as if you were really frightened. What happens now?

After a week or so of deliberately trying responses which are different from the usual pattern, you will probably notice that your tolerance for noise has increased tremendously— so much so that you won't consider it as noise any more.

Here's another modification of this "changing response" idea: suppose that a man and wife find that they are doing a lot of bickering. They don't particularly want to, but it

214

seems that so many of the little things that one does get on the other's nerves. And so they have little spats, a few harsh words and smoldering ill-feelings every day or so.

One way to minimize the ill-feelings and to clear the atmosphere is for them to have a little quarrel for a few minutes or so; then, by mutual agreement, they repeat the quarrel, but this time with the man saying all the things the wife said, and the wife making the remarks her husband made. In most cases, a few minutes of this reversal of role leads to a recognition of the ridiculousness of it all, and the tension of the scene dissolves in laughter.

These two ways of changing response might well be called "gimmicks"—they appear to be somewhat mechanical applications of a formula. This formula doesn't *always* work, but it works often enough to justify its being tried.

Let's see how the formula fits into the scheme of things as we have outlined it so far. To state our thesis again, every experience is made up of a complex pattern of sensations; the sensations are the elements which compose the experience, in the same way that bricks are the elements which compose a building. If we were to try to move—or change—an entire building, it would be extremely difficult. We can change it more easily by moving a brick at a time.

Similarly, when a person has a complex behavior pattern, it is not easy to alter the entire pattern at once, much easier to alter it one piece—that is, one sensation—at a time. By changing a single response-sensation, or by reversing a role, which carries with it different response-sensations, the entire structure of personality is thereby made more flexible.

215

This business of buildings and bricks, personality and sensation, is an analogy; it is an expression of one thought by comparing it with another. No analogy should be confused with the actuality. We *can* understand something better, however, as we compare it with numerous other things; in fact, as we said before, that is what we mean by understanding. Let us, therefore, make another analogy in the hope that it will be more clear.

Let's consider a caterpillar climbing up a tree. He comes to a branch, where he has a choice to make. He goes to the right or to the left. Whichever way he goes, he soon comes to another point of decision, then another, then another, until he is finally out to the leafy portion of the tree where he finds his food. With each decision he makes, it follows that he will find himself in a different portion of the tree; a right turn excludes his discovery of the left side of the tree, and so on.

We suggest that our sensations—our own feelings of love, hate, joy and sorrow, as well as our perception of sights, sounds and smells—are the signal for decision. They are also indicators that we have made a decision. If you, like the caterpillar, find that you have a rigid pattern of decision-making, such as always turning to the right, you can alter that pattern by being more observant of your own feelings. If you know that a branch is there, you can make whatever decision seems better; if you are unaware of the sensations which signal, "Here is a place where you can choose," you are acting as if you had no choice.

You can choose—and with every choice you open up new

fields of action for yourself. You don't have to go on, day after day, making the same sort of choices. As a matter of fact, you *don't* make the same choices; maybe it's always a right turn, but one time it's a turn onto a branch, another time a turn onto a twig, and so on. It is the awareness of choosing, of taking action, that gives us the sense of aliveness.

Recognizing that you can choose, that you have the power to make decisions, is one facet of happiness. The other idea that we want to leave with you is that happiness and knowledge of yourself go hand in hand.

We've already discussed this at length when we considered certain specific types of disease, but the implications are so important that a more general discussion might not be amiss.

We can know ourselves when we can know the sensations which are ourselves. The more we can feel, the more we can smell, the more we can taste—the more there is to us.

By expanding the horizons of our sensations we shall know better what goes on in the vast universe of which we are a part. We shall learn that we don't have to live in a case-hardened shell of knotted-up emotions. We shall learn that we don't have to fear our neighbors.

When we use our sensations as they can be used, we can look forward to each day with joy. It's a brand-new day! Maybe it will bring us a new joy—something really big and important like making a new friend, or enjoying the sheer beauty of the world around us. We can touch our loved ones, hold them close to us and feel the sweet warmth of their love. We can watch our children grow up and admire the ingenuity with which they learn to live. We can feel—we can laugh—we can cry, too.

Yes, even sorrow can be known and understood. When sorrow is recognized and experienced as it can be experienced, with unashamed tears, it will pass, leaving us the wiser for it. We shall find that only the hidden sorrow can hurt us and can breed more sorrow; grief that is told and shared with a friend becomes less grievous.

Every moment in life has an intensity all its own. We can feel it and make it ours forever—or we can blind ourselves, deafen ourselves, deaden all our senses until our living becomes a dull gray mockery of life.

We can choose to learn to be more alive, knowing that it's not an easy process, but recognizing that the rewards will more than repay the effort expended. There are experiences which, if we permit, can warp us into a practice for dying—but this doesn't have to happen. We can take the energies of these experiences and re-direct them into the path of living. Living can be joyful and good. We hope that you can find it so.

INDEX